*A Nineteenth-Century*
# ALGONQUIN ADVENTURE

*A Nineteenth-Century*

# ALGONQUIN ADVENTURE

James Dickson

*Edited and with an
Introduction and Notes by*

Gary Long

Fox Meadow Creations

Published by Fox Meadow Creations, Box 5401, Huntsville, ON P1H 2K7

CANADIAN CATALOGUING IN PUBLICATION DATA

Dickson, James, 1834-1926
A nineteenth-century Algonquin adventure

Originally published 1886 under title: Camping in the Muskoka region.
Includes bibliographical references and index.
ISBN 0-9681452-0-5

1. Canoes and canoeing – Ontario – Algonquin Provincial Park.
2. Camping – Ontario – Algonquin Provincial Park.
3. Algonquin Provincial Park (Ont.) – Description and travel.
1. Long, Gary. 11. Title. 111. Title: Camping in the Muskoka region.

FC3065.A65D52 1997      917.13'147      C97-930924-7
F1059.A4D52 1997

ILLUSTRATION CREDITS

*Front cover* – "High Falls" – woodblock print by Lorrie Szekat

*Opposite* – "James Dickson" – pencil sketch by Lorrie Szekat
*Based on a photograph from the Ministry of*
*Natural Resources; original taken c.1908*

*Page 12* – "Dickson's Algonquin" – map by Gary Long

# Contents

# Editor's Preface

IN 1886 THERE APPEARED IN PRINT AN UNPRETENTIOUS BOOK CALLED *Camping in the Muskoka Region*, by James Dickson. It was actually an account of a canoe trip on the Algonquin highlands. Beneath the often rustic prose lay an engaging narrative set in the rugged upland lake country that soon became the nucleus of Algonquin Park—Ontario's first and most famous provincial park.

Based on Dickson's experiences as a surveyor, but written as a story of a holiday fishing and canoe trip, *Camping in the Muskoka Region* was likely Canada's first book-length wilderness recreation guide. It enjoys added historical significance in light of Dickson's subsequent role in the establishment of the park, and because of its detailed description of virgin wilderness soon to be irrevocably altered by lumbering and other development.

In 1959 a new edition, subtitled *A Story of Algonquin Park* on the cover, was published by the Ontario Department of Lands and Forests. It closely followed the design of the original, and exactly replicated the text, but also included a map, six black-and-white photographs, and a foreword by Ontario premier Leslie M. Frost.

Now, with even the reprint unavailable except at a substantial premium on the used book market, it seemed time to publish another edition so the latest generation of Algonquin visitors could enjoy Dickson's informative and entertaining nineteenth-century adventure. But rather than once more simply reproduce the 1886 text, which had not been professionally edited, I decided to give it a modest polishing to weed out irrelevant bits and to coax a little more vigour and clarity from many of the passages. Some paragraph and chapter breaks have been adjusted, and modern spelling and punctuation conventions generally adopted. I've taken care, of course, to retain the flavour and particularly the meaning of Dickson's narrative. The relatively few factual errors remain (some I've noted separately).

I've given this edition a new title, to avoid confusion about the location. In 1886, "Algonquin" was not yet the term commonly applied to the region in which the book mostly takes place, but adjacent Muskoka was becoming well known and still conjured images of the wild north country. Today, even those who define "Muskoka" loosely would consider it distinct, in character and in location, from Algonquin.

James Dickson himself was an interesting man who, as noted, played a role in the founding of Algonquin Park. In the introduction, "James Dickson and Algonquin," I provide an overview of his life and *Camping in the Muskoka Region* in the context of the circumstances leading to the establishment of the park. Additional notes more specific to Dickson's story are grouped in one-page sections facing the opening of each of the chapters. These clarify points, provide additional background, and help bridge the gap of more than a century between Dickson's world and that familiar to the modern reader. Brief notations (such as the modern name for a geographical feature) are occasionally inserted in the text itself, in square brackets. An index and a bibliography, new features also in this edition, have been appended.

I should point that the introduction and the notes are optional: useful but not critical for the enjoyment of Dickson's story. Read them before or afterwards if the added background interests you.

The original *Camping in the Muskoka Region* contained just one interior illustration—in the 1880s few photographs or drawings of Algonquin scenes existed. Rather than use later pictures to capture the spirit of Dickson's Algonquin, I decided in this edition to let the text stand on its own. Dickson's vivid descriptions of the landscape need no support, and in any case there are lots of books bursting with great Algonquin pictures, both scenic and historical, for readers who like visual accompaniment (the bibliography lists some of these). The exceptions to the "no picture" decision are the sketch of Dickson facing the copyright page, and the woodblock print, *High Falls*, on the front cover, both by Lorrie Szekat. Dickson describes High Falls at some length in chapter 6.

Dickson's canoe route is easily traced on modern maps. Once the narrative enters what is now Algonquin Park (near the end of chapter 6), an excellent, inexpensive companion is the map *Canoe Routes of Algonquin Provincial Park*, published by the Friends of Algonquin Park. National topographic map sheet 31E (1:250,000 scale) covers the entire region encompassed by the book; it has the advantage of showing the topography and township boundaries mentioned by Dickson. I've included one map plate in this edition (page 12) to provide an overview of the countryside.

I would like to thank George Garland for letting me use his fragile original edition of *Camping in the Muskoka Region* as the text source, for pointing out research avenues, and for his observations based on long familiarity with the locale of the book and the history of Algonquin. Dan Strickland and Ron Tozer at the Algonquin Park Visitor Centre, W. J. Quinsey of the Association of Ontario Land Surveyors, and especially my parents, Marilyn and George Long, also provided valuable information and assistance.

Gary Long
*Huntsville, May 1997*

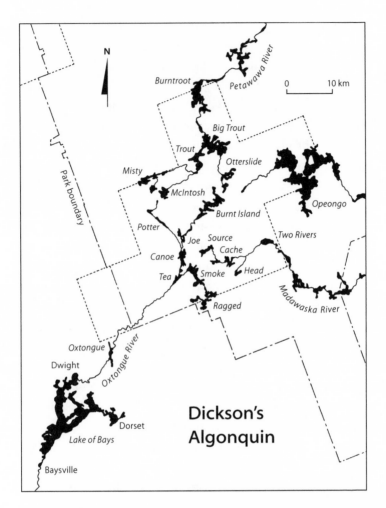

This map shows most of the Algonquin highland lakes and rivers canoed by the Dickson party in the book (also the downstream continuations, and Lake Opeongo, described but not visited). Dotted lines indicate the townships Dickson surveyed on the highlands 1878-1885: seven clustered in the south, and one, only partially on the map, in the northwest. The modern boundary of Algonquin Park is included for ease of putting the waterways in geographic context; the park wasn't created until 1893.

# James Dickson and Algonquin

WHEN JAMES DICKSON ARRIVED IN PRE-CONFEDERATION ONTARIO in 1841, at the age of 6, most of the population here lived in the arable southern portion of the province. To the north, between Georgian Bay and the Ottawa River, lay a vast dome of lake-strewn woodlands underlain by the ancient rocks of the Canadian Shield, uninhabited except for seasonal occupation by a few fur traders and Indians. Even the lumbermen in their insatiable quest for pine had only begun to penetrate the fringes of this wild and rugged country.

During the 1850s, population pressures and shortages of good farmland in the face of continuing immigration forced the government to begin expanding settlement into those unpopulated wilds. Erroneous reports by explorers had convinced many people that the impressive forests cloaking the hills of the region denoted fertile soils. Plans for new townships and an ambitious network of colonization roads in the territory were drawn up, and surveyors sent out to lay down the groundwork.

By the 1870s many of these plans were bearing fruit: drawn by the promise of free land, hundreds of settlers had moved into the southern part of the Shield in such areas as Muskoka, Haliburton, and sections of Renfrew and Hastings counties. Roads had been built, land cleared, farms established, villages founded. Buoyed by the apparent initial success of the northern settlement plans, the Ontario government decided that more Shield townships should be subdivided. From 1878 to 1885 James Dickson, now an experienced land surveyor, was hired to survey eight townships on the lofty uplands along the height of land between the Georgian Bay and the Ottawa River drainage—a region we know today as the Algonquin highlands. Some of this area was so remote that the lumbermen, steadily moving up the rivers tumbling from it, still had not touched an axe to extensive tracts of forest.

The experience of those eight years provided Dickson both the inspiration and the raw material for *Camping in the Muskoka Region*. And his knowledge of that area, combined with his reputation as a trustworthy surveyor and his interest in conservation, resulted in Dickson being chosen to participate in further activities leading to the establishment of the "Algonquin National Park of Ontario" on the highlands in 1893.

James Dickson was born in Scotland on October 30, 1834, *within sight of the battlefield of Flodden, 'where shriveled was fair Scotland's spier, and broken was her shield,'* as he wrote in an autobiographical sketch submitted to the Association of Ontario Land Surveyors in 1915 (he liked to salt his prose with quotations). After emigrating to Canada in 1841, the family established a farm in McNab Township in the Ottawa Valley, in the vicinity of the lower Madawaska River. At the time, this was on the fringe of settled territory near the edge of the Canadian Shield. Proximity to wilder country no doubt helped shaped Dickson's outlook and interests, for even as a youth he enjoyed exploring, fishing, and hunting.

Dickson worked on the farm until 1858, but not finding that particularly satisfying, he decided in spite of his own meagre formal education to become a teacher in adjacent Carleton County. Displaying his sense of humour and characteristic candour, not to mention resourcefulness, he wrote: *The very first day convinced me that some of the pupils were further advanced than I was myself. Here was a dilemma! But I was equal to the occasion. I had casually learned that my predecessor was in the habit of rushing the pupils too fast, so after a day or two, I told them that they were not sufficiently grounded in the rudiments, and it would be necessary for me to turn them back in some of the branches, and needless to say, I put them back far enough to be on par with my own qualifications, and I felt confident, that by earnest and close application, I could keep ahead of any of them.*

Teaching, or perhaps the remuneration ($220 a year), evidently proved not to his liking either; in January 1862 Dickson took a job as a surveyor's apprentice. In this work he found his true calling. By the spring of 1867 he had amassed enough training to pass his exams and become a fully qualified provincial land surveyor. Initially hanging out his shingle in the frontier hamlet of Minden, in Haliburton County, he moved south in 1869 to the thriving mill village of Fenelon Falls in the Kawartha Lakes district, making that his home and base of operations until his death in 1926. He married in 1873; three daughters survived infancy.

Dickson soon developed a reputation as an accurate, diligent, and efficient surveyor; that, along with his inherent honesty and reliability, always assured him of work. In addition to a busy local practice, he ranged far afield, conducting timber berth surveys for lumber companies and taking on numerous major assignments (mainly township surveys) for the Ontario and Canadian governments. As well, for ten years he served as Inspector of Surveys in Ontario. Dickson regarded surveying as more than just a job: he took a keen interest in raising the standards of the profession, which often left much to be desired in an era when rapid expansion of settlement created such demand for surveyors that even sloppy or incompetent ones could get work. For many years he actively took part in the affairs of the Association of Ontario Land

Surveyors. He joined the Association in 1887, was elected president in 1901, and participated in its functions well into his 80s.

The late 1880s and early 1890s, when he was involved in the Algonquin Park question, perhaps represented the zenith of Dickson's career. A fit man, both mentally and physically, he continued active work until quite an advanced age. He turned 70 in 1904 but the following year, after eight seasons of surveying on the Prairies, he signed on again as Inspector of Surveys in Ontario and spent three more rigorous years field-checking township surveys in the north. Closer to home, from 1908 to 1911 he undertook the risky task of determining compensation for people whose land had been flooded by dams on the Trent Canal. Many men had seen their reputations undeservedly tarnished as a result of political interference during the long corruption-plagued history of that project. When a Member of Parliament accused him of wrongdoing, Dickson immediately demanded an inquiry, conducted his own defence, and was completely exonerated—in his word, there was not a "tittle" of evidence against him.

Dickson was a meticulous and methodical man, which helps explain why a profession like surveying appealed to him, and why he proved competent at it. He set high standards for his own performance and expected the same from the men whose work he oversaw. With his great practical knowledge of surveying and of the natural landscape, he would have been an interesting man to work with, and a pleasant companion too, for though stern and conservative in his views—he was a staunch Presbyterian—he was a congenial fellow with a dry sense of humour. Some measure of his personality is evident in his naming of two small lakes, Fools and Error, along one of his survey lines on the Algonquin highlands. In *Names of Algonquin*, George Garland suggests these might have been a result of some mistake, presumably an avoidable one, by a member of the survey party. It would certainly appeal to

Dickson's sense of humour, and to his sense of justice, to provide the unfortunate individual with a long-lasting reminder of his incompetence (the names surveyors applied to features often survived, due to the official nature of the plans they appeared on).

Aside from technical competence, a prerequisite for a surveyor, especially in earlier days, was a love of the outdoors, and it is clear that in adulthood Dickson thoroughly enjoyed hunting, fishing, canoeing, and camp life in general. Judging by the book, he had a particular weakness for fresh trout! His surveys of the Algonquin highland townships from 1878 to 1885 provided an ideal marriage of his professional and recreational interests. Although the surveying itself involved long hours under often gruelling conditions, there was always time to gaze out over the hills, enjoy an evening pipe by the lakeside, and of course the Sabbath—the only day of rest—provided opportunity to amble through the woods or cast a line into a promising trout pool.

A township survey entailed dividing the land into concessions and 100-acre farm lots by means of an intersecting grid of lines spaced just over two kilometres apart. In a typical township this meant some 200 kilometres to be traversed with compass and chain (the latter for measuring distances) and cut out with axes. Imagine the enormous difficulty of running these straight lines on the rugged Canadian Shield: all those intervening lakes, rivers, swamps, cliffs, hills, and dense woods that had to be conquered or circumvented. Little wonder that it usually took several months to complete a single township. During this time the surveyor and his party—assistant, cook, axemen, and chainmen—camped out in the wilderness, surviving on a diet largely of beans and salt pork (typical bush camp fare of the era) supplemented by whatever fish and game they could catch or shoot. To succeed on these jobs a surveyor needed to be in top condition and an expert woodsman, not to mention well organized and an effective leader.

Besides subdividing the township, the surveyor was expected to explore and map the major rivers and lakes, and report on the natural attributes of the countryside—timber, topography, soils, geology, navigable waters, waterpower sites, anything that might influence future settlement and economic development.

Most of the eight highland townships Dickson surveyed were readily accessible in summer only by canoe. Food and gear for the entire survey season had to be conveyed by steamboat and wagon, and on the backs of the men, to a river flowing from the region, then laboriously paddled and portaged upstream. Given the distances involved, and the quantity of supplies, this task could take two or more weeks before work could even begin. Typically, field work commenced in June or July and continued until fall.

Seven of Dickson's townships, forming the locale of *Camping in the Muskoka Region*, sprawl contiguously across the headwaters of the Muskoka, Petawawa, and Madawaska rivers. For these, the southwesterly-flowing Oxtongue River provided Dickson with the most convenient access. A headwater of the Muskoka, it drops off the highlands into Lake of Bays in eastern Muskoka District. It had been long-used by Indians, explorers, and others as a canoe route up to the height of land, and thence into the headwaters of the eastward-flowing Madawaska and Petawawa rivers. Chains of lakes entwining the hills in the headwaters of all three streams provide easy canoe routes through much of the uplands.

Dickson was surveying the country as a prelude to agricultural settlement, but his reports indicate that, overall, he considered less than a quarter of it arable—and even that was using an optimistic definition of farmable land. Like many surveyors, he apparently overestimated the fertility of the thin glacial tills of the Shield, capable of growing impressive forests but quickly depleted when placed under cultivation. For instance, in 1881 he reported that more than forty percent of Hunter Township was "well adapted" for settlement. This hilly township, stretching from Joe Lake north to Misty, is certainly not what comes to mind when you think of farmland! Dickson's assessment of Peck Township (Tea–Smoke–Canoe Lake district) in 1880 gives a more realistic idea of farming potential on the highlands: *I regret to say that I found very little good land in the township, not more than between five and six thousand acres.* (Peck covers almost 50,000 acres.)

Dickson certainly recognized the lumbering potential of the region, noting vast quantities of the coveted pine growing in the virgin forests at the headwaters of the rivers, particularly the Oxtongue River: *The pine still untouched lies mainly adjacent to the Muskoka waters, and will make a valuable timber limit* (McLaughlin Township report, 1883); *the pine especially around Joe Lake* [is] *of a large and superior quality* (Hunter Township, 1881). At a government auction in 1892, the Gilmour lumber company paid record prices for the rights to cut this timber; likely, Dickson's reports initially sparked the firm's interest in the region.

Sprinkled through Dickson's reports too are comments on the beauty of the lakes and the abundance of fish and game—for instance, from his 1880 Peck Township report, *the lakes* [are] *very beautiful, with deep clear water and teeming with speckled and salmon trout.* These suggest Dickson had quickly begun to appreciate the outstanding value of the region for recreation. Not only was this forested lake country exceptionally scenic, with splendid canoeing, camping, and fishing opportunities, it was fairly close to the population centres of southern Ontario—attributes as important now as they were more than a century ago. Near the end of his 1884 report on Bishop Township, Dickson writes: *It is a matter of surprise that so few tourists and seekers after romantic scenery visit the head waters of the Muskoka, Petewawa and Madawaska Rivers. They are only a short distance from the settlement and easily accessible by canoes, and the portages on the Muskoka are of a trifling character, while every bend of the river unfolds some new beauty of mountain, forest or stream; while the lakes, though not as large as those further down, are unrivalled for beauty of scenery, and it may literally be called a sportsman's paradise, the woods abounding with moose and red deer, bear, wolves, and the various fur-bearing animals, the lakes and large creeks with the largest and palatable varieties of speckled and salmon trout, which can be had in abundance either by fishing with the hook and line, or by setting the night line, at all seasons of the year.*

The highlands had clearly captivated Dickson. That they would inspire this 50-year-old, rather pragmatic surveyor with limited schooling to write a book amply demonstrates the power of the Algonquin magic.

Dickson may have begun *Camping in the Muskoka Region* in 1884. That year he finished surveying all the townships that provide the setting (with the exception of Bower, the most easterly, and the portions of that one described in the story seem an afterthought, as though inserted after the narrative had already been roughed out). We certainly know that the theme of the book had crystallized in his mind by then. In many ways unique, *Camping in the Muskoka Region* nonetheless represented just a part of a new genre emerging in Canada in response to changing attitudes and economic times—the scenic guidebook.

The 1870s and 1880s saw unprecedented expansion of activity in Canada. Settlement pushed north into the wilds of the Canadian Shield in Ontario, and the Canadian Pacific Railway headed west to the mountains and the Pacific. Great interest was generated in what lie beyond the settled eastern parts of the country, especially among an increasingly sophisticated urban population beginning to view the natural environment as a place of potential enjoyment and spiritual renewal rather than, as the pioneers saw it, an enemy to conquer. Numerous books and articles filled with beautiful drawings and poetic descriptions of wild scenery were published, devoured by a public eager to learn about, if not visit, the constantly unfolding wonders of their young country (one splendid example was *Picturesque Canada*). These publications, however, tended to concentrate more on areas accessible by steamboat or railway and assumed the traveller would stay in hotels or inns; less was said of the more inaccessible spots, and nothing of Dickson's own paradise on the Algonquin highlands, where the traveller had to rely on his muscles for locomotion and on his own cooking, hunting, and fishing prowess for sustenance.

Addressing the latter deficiency, *Camping in the Muskoka Region* rolled off the press in 1886. In it Dickson writes, *it is the purpose of the present writer to visit the hitherto unknown wilds of the upper Muskoka [River], and endeavour to lay before his readers some of the beauties of lake and river, of mountain and valley, which, though almost at our doors, are still so far away and so little known.*

The book bears the imprint of the Toronto firm of C. Blackett Robinson, but likely they just produced the book, with Dickson actually the publisher. A modest 164-page paperbound volume, about 5½ by 8¼ inches, *Camping in the Muskoka Region* was unillustrated except for a small wood engraving on the front cover and a second as frontispiece. The latter, captioned *On North River* (the name for the Oxtongue in Dickson's day), shows a canoe on a placid forest-lined stream and could have been a scene on the lower river near Lake of Bays—a section, ironically, bypassed by Dickson. The other, *A Landing Place*, depicts a typical northern lakeside scene that was probably not on the Algonquin highlands. Artwork and photographs featuring Algonquin scenes, especially in the parts Dickson traversed, simply were not available in the mid-1880s. But although Dickson was not a professional writer, his text captures the spirit and magnificence of the lakes and hills in a manner that renders illustration superfluous.

The narrative of some 49,000 words describes a month-long canoe trip, apparently in July and August 1885, by a party of at least nine men in birchbark canoes. The route, up the Oxtongue River then branching out through the headwaters of that stream and those of the Petawawa and Madawaska rivers, coincides with what today are some of the most popular Algonquin canoe routes, and several of the lakes visited are familiar ones along the Highway 60 corridor. The route also coincides, very precisely, with the territory Dickson covered in his township surveys. As Dickson would not have had time to make a summer pleasure trip of such duration because of his survey work, it is certain the canoe trip is based on incidents and observations from the survey expeditions of 1878-1885. Dickson canoed every stream and lake described, camped on most spots the holiday party did, and perhaps even caught as many trout as he claimed! He clearly casts himself as narrator; he is likely the "Jim" with the big legs hogging the bed in chapter 3. In the foreword to the 1959 edition, Leslie M. Frost suggests "Sam" was Samuel Barr of Fenelon Falls, Dickson's preferred cook on his surveys (a good, reliable cook was essential to the success of the field work).

Frost notes too that Dickson's daughter Agnes told him she could not recall her father ever taking a holiday—added evidence that *Camping in the Muskoka Region* is a composite story. Several minor discrepancies in the text also suggest that Dickson did a "cut and paste" job to create the impression of a single trip. For instance, the first day of the expedition, on which the party purchases supplies, mills are operating, and liquor is available, proves to be a Sunday if you count back from the next "Sabbath" mentioned. Children were in school, too (an observation deleted from this edition): this was possible in July in pioneer days, but not on Sunday! Interesting also is the way the supply of food and gear appears to expand as the story progresses, far beyond what was listed at the beginning—although much of this Dickson may have taken for granted and merely did not bother to enumerate at the outset.

But for all of that, it is a convincing narrative, full of the little details that lend authenticity. Dickson's writing style, despite some clumsiness, is direct and immediate: you really feel you are right there with him, paddling and portaging across the highlands, dining on salt pork and fresh trout, braving stormy waters and pesky black flies, and enjoying the scenery *in all its varied beauty* (one of Dickson's pet phrases). Dickson undoubtedly had assistance writing the book. A couple of parts deviate too far from the style of his unedited survey reports to have been his alone, even allowing for the extra effort presumably expended on the project.

Given his profession, it is not surprising that Dickson describes the route in such detail that it can be precisely traced, even where portage alignments have changed and dams have radically altered water levels—only a surveyor would note the crossing of every township boundary! Abundant information intended originally as practical advice and instruction for novice canoe trippers and campers contrasts sharply with modern wilderness practice: how to paddle and repair birchbark canoes, construct a pack with blankets, make balsam-bough beds, catch trout by night line, and cook salt pork, beans, venison stew, apple sauce, and other fare—pretty much everything you needed to know to set out into the wilds in the late nineteenth century. A hard-working man of simple tastes, Dickson is disdainful of the creature comforts and city food that some canoe trippers take on their expeditions, then return home *vainly hugging the notion they have been 'roughing it.'* Other than that they were not surveying, Dickson's holiday party was virtually indistinguishable from a working survey crew of those times.

Of great interest to readers both in the 1880s and today, Dickson's narrative contains detailed description of the forests, scenery,

waterways, and fish and wildlife. There are a few errors and mis-
conceptions, but the general level of accuracy is very good, and
certainly reflective of Dickson's observational abilities. Touching
also on some history of the Algonquin highlands—lumbering and
trapping, mainly—*Camping in the Muskoka Region* can be regarded
as the first Algonquin guidebook; indeed, it appears to have been
the first book to describe the art of wilderness canoe tripping and
camping for the pleasure tripper—at least for the pleasure tripper
willing to endure Dickson's spartan notion of the activity.

Although quasi-fictional, the book contains valuable information about the state of the landscape and human activity on the
Algonquin highlands in the early 1880s. At that time an island of
wilderness still existed straddling the height of land, untouched by
the lumbermen working their way up the river systems. Much of
this territory underwent tremendous changes just a few years later
with the arrival of lumbermen and construction across the highlands of lumber baron J.R. Booth's Ottawa, Arnprior and Parry
Sound Railway. Ascending the Madawaska valley past Lake of Two
Rivers, Cache, and Source lakes, then crossing into the Oxtongue
watershed and skirting Joe Lake before running up the valley of
Potter Creek, the railway passed through the heart of the region
Dickson surveyed. Dickson's description of the countryside under
natural conditions is thus an important historical record.

Dickson frequently comments on the fish, birds, and mammals
of the Algonquin highlands, often in connection with catching or
shooting them in a manner we would now consider irresponsible.
But that behaviour must be compared to the norms of the day:
Dickson was actually a proponent of wildlife conservation, highly
critical of the way the white man indiscriminately slaughtered
game. He touches on this theme often enough that it might be
regarded as a secondary reason he wrote and published the book.
In mentioning the idea of wildlife preserves on lands unsuited for

agriculture (perhaps with the Algonquin highlands in mind), he echoed a theme growing among Ontario hunters and anglers by the mid-1880s. Indeed, by then the idea of conserving wildlife as well as other natural resources was taking root both inside and outside of government. Events that would lead in just a few years to the establishment of Algonquin Park were already well under way, and Dickson was about to be thrust onto centre stage.

The attitude of the white inhabitants of Canada towards their environment through most of the nineteenth century was overwhelmingly one of *conquer!* Chop down the forests, plough the land, establish towns and industries, build roads, canals, and railways. The country seemed so vast, its natural resources so limitless, that many people thought exploitation and development could continue almost in perpetuity.

By late in the century this idea was crumbling under the pressure of the reality of decades of destructive environmental and resource exploitation practices. In particular, the removal of forests in eastern Canada by settlers and fire was beginning to cause serious problems: erosion, flooding, insufficient summer stream flows to run mills, loss of wildlife habitat, and of course the potential collapse of the vital forestry industry. Unregulated hunting and fishing, combined with habitat destruction, had seriously depleted stocks of fish and game. At the same time, an increasingly urban population was becoming more cognizant of, and enjoying, the natural splendour and recreational opportunities of the country's lands and waters—as noted earlier, beginning to view Nature as a friend, not a foe. Taking all these factors together, it is understandable that a conservation movement arose and began to lobby the government for remedial action.

Conservationists in the late nineteenth century represented a spectrum of backgrounds, philosophies, and objectives. The need to maintain forested regions for lumbering and watershed protection was one important emerging theme, while a large influential group that included the hunting and angling interests saw wildlife conservation as the primary goal. One idea that most seemed to endorse was that an extensive tract of forested land be set aside as a park or reserve, as had already occurred in Quebec and in the United States. In the 1880s strong pressure was brought to bear on the Ontario government to do just that; some of this came from within the civil service itself.

It appears that the first person to propose reserving lands for conservation specifically on the Algonquin highlands was Robert Phipps, forestry clerk in the Ontario Department of Agriculture. Hired to educate farmers in the need to maintain woodlots, he recognized the economic role of forests as well as the desirability of retaining them in the source areas of river systems to help regulate stream flows. In 1884 he recommended that the government set aside a large block of forest in the headwaters of several rivers on the uplands between the Ottawa River and Georgian Bay, to be closed to settlement and maintained for timber production and watershed conservation. Lumber companies supported the idea: it would assure them both of wood and of water in the streams to float the timber out of the wilderness.

Alexander Kirkwood, chief clerk in the land sales section of the Department of Crown Lands, liked the idea too. In 1885 he suggested to crown lands commissioner Timothy Pardee that a block be set aside as the "Algonkin Forest and Park," to serve not only for watershed protection and timber harvesting, but also as a wildlife sanctuary and for recreation. In 1886, the year Dickson brought out *Camping in the Muskoka Region*, Kirkwood published his recommendations, apparently with the approval of Pardee as a means of gauging reaction to the idea from interest groups and the public. Since Dickson worked for the Department of Crown

Lands on the township surveys, he may have known what was going on, and perhaps even received encouragement in his own complementary publishing endeavour.

Kirkwood's recommendations, no doubt assisted by Dickson's evocative descriptions, generated much favourable response from lumber companies, conservation groups, and those interested in wildlife protection. As a result, in 1887 Pardee asked Dickson to prepare a detailed report on the area, with particular reference to its suitability as a park. Some townships on the highlands had not yet been surveyed: the government wanted to be sure these did not have good agricultural or other potential.

Dickson was a logical choice for this task. Through his previous work he was already familiar with much of the region, and he had proved a reliable, knowledgeable, and trustworthy person. And of course from his book, and probably from conversation as well, it was clear that Dickson would favourably view a park. Pardee, also sympathetic to the idea, was probably happier to see someone of like mind up there. Another factor was that Dickson had to visit Algonquin again anyway in 1887, as part of his new job as Inspector of Surveys. Four Algonquin highland townships, north and east of the ones he had surveyed, were due for his scrutiny. It was convenient, while he was up there, to have a look at the whole area. Dickson tackled the assignment with enthusiasm. As an ally of the wildlife conservation movement, he must have relished the chance to make important recommendations related to that issue.

Of course little of the Algonquin highlands was suited for cultivation—less than ten percent, Dickson reported in January 1888, and even that was in widely scattered bits (Audrey Saunders provides summary and excerpts from his report in *Algonquin Story.*) Dickson wholeheartedly supported the park idea, recommending that eleven townships be set aside for the purpose. He accorded wildlife conservation high priority: *The preservation from destruction of moose, deer and beaver would, in my opinion, alone warrant the Government in making this a reservation.* The park could act as a wildlife reservoir, providing a natural outflow of game to replenish stocks in the surrounding territory.

Dickson saw no problem with continued logging. In his view, the resulting second-growth forest would be more productive wildlife habitat. To aid lumber companies in floating their timber down the rivers, he advocated the construction of reserve dams in the headwaters. He failed to recognize, like many others then, the destructive impact of dams and log driving on fish habitat and spawning beds.

Besides describing the geography and resources, Dickson made a number of practical recommendations for the management and use of the proposed park. Much of this centred on wildlife management, but not surprisingly, he also emphasized the recreational potential of the region, making detailed suggestions for an illustrated guidebook and comprehensive map to aid visitors, who he assumed would reach the park by canoeing up the rivers as he himself had been doing. Evidently he thought the park should remain largely undeveloped for people who wanted to "rough it." Kirkwood, on the other hand, had proposed leasing some land for cottages and a lodge.

Dickson was too pragmatic to raise the possibility of preserving even a small section of the highlands as wilderness. Although lumbering obviously had a significant impact on the scenery and the environment, he made no negative comments on that aspect of the activity (in a survey reports he criticizes wasteful logging practices, but it was the waste, not the effects, that bothered him). A strong adherent to the multiple-use philosophy of resource utilization, he would have regarded it a crime to just let the forest stand there when it contained valuable timber. The woodlands could serve both lumberman and pleasure seeker.

Dickson's report, added to the considerable weight of all the other interests continuing to clamour for a park, impelled Pardee to have Alexander Kirkwood draw up a draft "Algonkin Forest and Park Act" in 1888. Then the process stalled, at least on that front. Pardee took sick and was replaced as crowns lands commissioner by Arthur Hardy, who did not regard the park as a priority. However, in 1890, to appease growing public agitation about the sad state of Ontario's fish and game stocks, the government did set up a Royal Commission on Fish and Game. In February 1892 that body released a report blasting the government for mismanagement of fish and wildlife. Among its many recommendations it called for establishment of a provincial game park.

Recognizing broad public support for a park, the government resurrected the Phipps–Kirkwood–Dickson idea for one on the Algonquin highlands. Within days of receiving the fish and game report, it set up a Royal Commission on Forest Reservation and National Park to determine which lands were best suited and to recommend details of the plan. Along with Alexander Kirkwood, Robert Phipps, and two other civil servants, James Dickson was appointed a member. Dickson was certainly the leading authority on the region. During the preceding fourteen years he had traversed it more extensively than just about anyone else.

The commission was hardly an independent one—or even a necessary one. In *Protected Places: A History of Ontario's Provincial Parks System*, Gerald Killan takes the view that it was really just a way of dressing up a decision already taken, and a delaying tactic to give the government time to auction off the remaining pine timber berths on the Algonquin highlands (that took place on October 13, 1892). Certainly the five commissioners did fulfil an important function in pooling their expertise and research efforts to develop specific recommendations, but they were already on the government payroll, much of the background material had

previously been collected, and the outcome was virtually a fore-
gone conclusion. Royal commission status was scarcely essential
to the task; indeed, the commission formally met just twice.

The first of those meetings did not occur until November
1892 (*after* the timber berths had been auctioned off, Killan notes).
Dickson, however, had begun working on the project as early as
March. On instructions from Arthur Hardy, he journeyed several
times to the Algonquin highlands to collect additional information and to closely examine the unsurveyed townships of Sproule
and Preston. As the field man, it was his job to supply data about
the proposed park area.

The commission completed its report early in 1893 and submitted it in March. Dickson's most noticeable contribution was a
detailed description of the geography and resources of the region
(right down to the islands "literally blue with huckleberries"). As
expected, the report contained no surprises. It reaffirmed the lack
of agricultural potential on the highlands and recommended that
eighteen townships be set aside as "Algonquin National Park."
Watershed protection, wildlife conservation, and recreation would
be the prime objectives. The lumber companies could continue to
cut mature pine timber.

The government wasted no time implementing the recommendations, pushing the park enabling Act through the legislature
in May with little opposition. *No scheme ever conceived by any government in any part of the Dominion has met with such general approval.
All shades of politicians seemed to unite for once in its favor,* Dickson
observed in an article "Ontario's Big Game" (*Canadian Magazine*,
November 1894, quoted in *Protected Places*).

Dickson's role in the founding of one of Canada's great parks
was a fine achievement for the hard-working rural surveyor, but
widespread recognition of Dickson's contribution, especially his
groundwork in the 1880s (much more important than the royal

commission), did not come until the 1940s when the Department of Lands and Forests commissioned Audrey Saunders to research and write *Algonquin Story*.

In the summer of 1893 Dickson journeyed to the new Algonquin Park. Again the most logical choice, he had been asked to act as guide and advisor for the first chief ranger, Peter Thomson. After leading the party up the Oxtongue River, he helped select a site for a park headquarters on Canoe Lake, then took Thomson and one of his rangers on a tour of the waterways to familiarize them with the territory and to suggest locations for shelter huts to be used on patrols. Returning again to the park later in August, perhaps for the last time using his old familiar canoe route up the Oxtongue, Dickson spent better than a month surveying part of the south boundary.

Dickson must have had mixed emotions that summer. True, his beloved lakelands now lay in a great park to be enjoyed ultimately by millions of visitors; but the hand of the lumberman was now reaching into the last bastion of wilderness. Even as pragmatic a man as he must surely have felt a twinge of regret at the impending assault on the virgin forests along the height of land. As he canoed through the Oxtongue headwaters, the Gilmour lumber company was busy building camps, dams, and roads in the region. Come winter, the ring of axes would echo between the hills, and the giant pines would come crashing to earth. For most people, *Camping in the Muskoka Region* would provide the final glimpse of that last piece of "primeval" landscape. Dickson at least had his memories. Algonquin would never be the same again.

# James Dickson's Narrative

CHAPTER I NOTES *Just the year before* Camping in the Muskoka Region *came out, the completion of the Canadian Pacific Railway truly made Canada a great, united country. The excitement of that national project, and the well-publicized splendour of the western mountains, somewhat overshadowed the more modest landscape of the Algonquin highlands, yet probably only made Dickson more determined to tell people about his "sylvan retreat" virtually in the back yard of the most heavily populated part of the country.*

*From this opening chapter, nearly 2000 words describing rivers of the Prairies and the plight of Prairie Indians have been edited out. This material is scarcely essential to the theme of the book, and it's not clear why Dickson included it—or even if he wrote it. The style differs noticeably from his own. Almost certainly it was written by his unidentified assistant. Dickson's parents, brothers, and sister moved to Manitoba in the early 1880s; that could explain the Prairie connection. Dickson might have gone out there to help them in his "off season."*

*The last section of the Introductory opened chapter 2 in the original edition. Dickson was quite familiar with the lakes of Muskoka District mentioned. He passed through Muskoka each year on his journeys to and from the Algonquin highlands. Although still very much a frontier, with lumbering and subsistence farming the main economic activities, by the 1880s the region was becoming a popular destination for summer vacationers and sportsmen, in part due to rail access and to steamboat service on many lakes. Descriptions and drawings of Muskoka scenery featured prominently in numerous publications of that era.*

*The recognition factor of Muskoka may have influenced Dickson's choice of title for his book (it appears, from the running head in the 1886 edition, that he first chose the less specific* Camp Life in Northern Ontario*). Or perhaps he considered the "Muskoka Region" to encompass the watershed of the Muskoka River, which extends considerably eastwards from Muskoka up onto the Algonquin highlands and is the locale of the greater part of the narrative.*

I

## *Introductory*

———◆●◆———

IN THESE DAYS OF STEAMBOATS, RAILWAYS, TOURISTS, AND NEWSPAPER correspondents, one would think there ought to be few spots now in this Ontario of ours a *terra incognita*, few spots that either the pen of the traveller has not described or the pencil of the artist not illustrated and brought vividly before the mind's eye of those who have not had the opportunity of seeing for themselves. Still, there are many grand scenes of lake and river, of mountain and valley, of wimpling burn and brawling brook, of lovely forest glade and fern-fringed dell, that have been neither described nor illustrated.

The pen and pencil of a Butler have vividly depicted the Great Lone Land and the Wild North Land; those of a Grant, a Cheadle, a Milton, and a Pellesier embellished and brought to every fireside the snow-capped summits of the Rocky Mountains and the dark canyons and lonely valleys of the Fraser and Thompson rivers. The newspaper correspondent and the artist have followed in the train of a Governor-General across that vast country, our great North-West, and painted in glowing colours its fertile plains and majestic rivers, prophesied the great future in store for it. Other writers and artists have accompanied another Viceroy across the continent, and published the grandeur of the Pacific slope. Gentlemen of the same ilk have followed the railway engineers up the valley of the mighty Ottawa, round the base of the towering Laurentian Hills north of lakes Huron and Superior, across the great prairie belt, down the dark canyons and gulches of the Rocky Mountains to the shore of the Pacific Ocean, and have in glowing language described the varied beauties and great extent of country.

But while the descriptive powers of so many pens and pencils have been employed in describing the magnificence of that vast land, there are scenes of equal, if not greater, beauty almost at our doors, where though the extent of country is not so great, nor the streams so majestic, there are many fairy nooks, lakes and islands, rolling rivers and tumbling brooks, pine-clad hills and lovely forest dells, that would task the powers of the most gifted pen to describe or pencil to illustrate. Here the waters are clear as crystal, and so cool and refreshing that the very sight tempts one to taste the draught. Here almost every little creek can provide the hungry with a rich repast of brook trout, while every lake teems with luscious speckled lake and salmon trout, which can be caught in abundance either by angling or by the night line in all seasons of the year. Here the lakes and rivers abound with the beaver, mink, and otter, the woods with the marten, fisher, and fox, the graceful red deer and gigantic noble moose, and the lynx, grey wolf, and black bear.

Come with me and we will spend a summer holiday in this sylvan retreat where, though we can reach it in a few hours travel, we will be completely cut off from the busy haunts of men.

The lakes of the lower Muskoka River—Muskoka, Rosseau, and Joseph—have been explored in every nook and corner, their every bay and inlet, solitary rock and pine-clad islet graphically described. The best spots to secure the denizens of their depths, and the islets where the basket can be most quickly filled with the luscious huckleberry, raspberry, and strawberry, have been pointed out to the sportsman and the berry picker. Lakes Mary, Fairy, Vernon, and Peninsula, and the winding river between, have also afforded material for pen and pencil. One or two of the more venturesome newspaper correspondents have hazarded a few lines on the beauties of Lake of Bays and Hollow Lake, but it is the purpose of the present writer to visit the hitherto unknown wilds of the upper Muskoka River, and endeavour to lay before his readers some of the beauties of lake and river, of mountain and valley, which though almost at our doors are still so far away and so little known.

CHAPTER 2 NOTES    *Today, cars and paved highways make access to Algonquin a swift and easy matter. In the early 1880s, getting there was a rigorous adventure in itself, demanding considerable effort and certainly far more than the "few hours" suggested in chapter 1.*

*Dickson begins his account with the party arriving in Bracebridge by steamboat (probably on the sidewheeler* Nipissing*). In 1886 the railway opened north through the village, but before then, travellers could journey by train only as far as Gravenhurst at the foot of the Muskoka Lakes. A fleet of steamboats made regular runs around these big lakes and up the Muskoka River to the head of navigation at Bracebridge, a busy commercial centre in the heart of the Free Grant lands of Muskoka.*

*A bone-jarring wagon ride eastwards along a primitive road (Highway 117 now) brings the party to Baysville at the foot of huge Lake of Bays. Here the men stay overnight at a hotel—perhaps Baysville House, overlooking the dam and later called Lincoln Lodge, "the best place to eat by a dam site." Another steamboat carries them 23 kilometres up the lake to Dwight and close to the Oxtongue River, their canoe route to the highlands (the river was called the North back then). Known today for its cottages and resorts, Lake of Bays in the early 1880s was the domain of lumbermen, scattered settlers, and a few sportsmen. Dwight, so named in 1885, was a mere hamlet on the fringe of wilderness; the "Temperance House" Dickson mentions was the boarding house–post office–store owned by Edmund J. Gouldie, the original settler there. A picnic lunch of hardtack and salt pork ("long clear bacon") at Dwight strongly suggests Henrietta's Pine Bakery was not yet in operation!*

*Dickson was misguided in his enthusiasm for subsistence farming in the rugged countryside. With his conservative outlook and strong work ethic, he admired those who showed initiative and laboured hard. Unfortunately, even the most diligent "hardy pioneer" often failed when pitted against the stony, infertile soils of the Canadian Shield.*

*The wood pigeon noted on page 40 is a passenger pigeon. This once-abundant species, now extinct, was still present here in the early 1880s.*

## 2

## *Preparing for a Start*

WE LEAVE THE STEAMER AT THE THRIVING VILLAGE OF BRACEBRIDGE, to retrace her route with deck load of pleasure seekers down the winding river to Muskoka Lake, across to Port Carling, through the locks and up the short stream into Lake Rosseau, then thread her mazy course amongst the scrub oak, pine, and fern-clad islets to her nightly quarters at the village of Rosseau.

Securing the frugal supply of provisions necessary for our sojourn in the wilds, we engage a team of horses and wend our way eastwards through a newly settled district, past little churches and unpretentious schoolhouses, past the trough-covered shanty, the more substantial hewn-log house with shingled roof, and the occasional frame dwelling of the hardy settler. We pass through stately groves of sugar maple, of balsam, and of birch, beech, and basswood; through stretches of woods where the fire-fiend has left his trademark on giant pine and hemlock and destroyed many thousands of dollars of valuable timber; through sections depleted of their timber by the axe of the lumberman; through tamarack, spruce, and cedar swamps; through clearings of waving grain and new-mown hay. Herd of kine quietly feed on the luxuriant grass that has sprung up along the old lumber roads, and the tinkle of the cowbell is heard on every side. We pass over stretches of hard clay and soft sandy road; up stony hills where the horses must strain every nerve to haul their load to the top, down others where it is equally difficult, even with the assistance of a brake on the wheel, to restrain the impetus of the vehicle; over corduroys in swamps and morasses; up an inclined plane through the Devil's Gap; over strongly built bridges spanning impassable gullies with their ever-present grass and alder-fringed creek beneath.

Now the timid grey rabbit bounds along the road before us; again, a mother partridge hurries her down-covered chicks to cover. High overhead, the grey hen-hawk basks in the sunshine, giving forth its shrill whistle at short intervals, while the coo of the wood pigeon, the chirr of the squirrel, and the cluck of the striped chipmunk are heard in the neighbouring covert, and from yonder beetling crag an antlered buck gazes down upon our lumbering wagon with its gay and chattering load.

After some sixteen miles of jolting over the rough road, with occasional short walks up the hills to ease the panting horses, we make a sudden bend to the right and enter the busy little village of Baysville, on the north bank of the south branch of the Muskoka River. The village is some two miles below the foot of Lake of Bays, or as some call it, Trading Lake, and is the end of steamboat navigation in this quarter. Here there is a fine water power spanned by a substantially built bridge, dam, and timber slide; on the north side is a sawmill, and on the south a grist or flour mill, both doing a thriving trade. Out on one of the piers a disciple of Izaak Walton hauls the speckled beauties from the seething waters that rush and tumble over the dark granite rocks.

Here we pause for the night in one of the hotels, presided over by a courteous landlord and attentive landlady, and sup at a board loaded with dainties that would tempt the most fastidious epicure, and retire to a comfortable room and a bed that would woo the drowsy god even if we had not the aching joints occasioned by our long and rough ride. This is the last night we shall pass between wooden walls and under shingled roof-tree for, it may be, several weeks. Tomorrow night, and for many succeeding, we shall sleep beneath our cotton tent, our bed the fragrant boughs of balsam, and instead of snow-white sheets and feather pillows, we will lie between the folds of our strong grey blankets with—shall we mention it?—our boots and folded coat for a pillow.

Tonight we may indulge in brown stout, Bass's ale, and other strong drinks; fragrant Havana; tea, with both cream and sugar; tarts, pies, jellies, and puddings; and fresh eggs and luscious butter just from the churn. Tomorrow our only drink will be tea—in a tin pannikin, with neither cream nor sugar—or the pure crystal water of the river, for no intoxicants of any kind are to be found in our commissariat. Biscuits, or hardtack, as they are familiarly called, with pork, beans, and dried apples, and perhaps a bottle of pickles or box of sardines for the first meal or two, shall compose our food, while to smoke aught but a briarroot or clay pipe is a forbidden luxury in our camp. Here we must complete our supplies. Our birchen canoes are to be purchased; a few forgotten articles, such as an extra tin dish, a box of matches, a little baking soda, and an extra plug or two of Myrtle Navy, must likewise be added to our store; also a few bottles of painkiller, a bottle of castor oil and a box or two of pills, and a few cakes of Castile soap.

Early in the morning the shrill whistle of the little steamer awakes us from our dreams, and in a few minutes we are up and dressed. It is a glorious morning. The rays of the rising sun shine on the dark green woods to the west, while the red face of old Sol himself peeks above an eastern hill. A thin mist only partially conceals the rushing river. The sharp buzz of the saw is already to be heard converting the huge pine log into lumber. The disciple of Walton is again at his post with rod and fly, bent on securing his breakfast of shiny beauties hidden beneath the surface of the bubbling waters. The whistling of birds mingles with the joyous song of the trim milkmaid as she seats herself by the side of old Hawkie to extract the rich milk from the distended udder. Gay Chanticleer struts round, leading the feathered beauties of his harem with their young brood in search of the proverbial early worm. A stray lady porker with her squalling brood trudges about on the lookout for the easiest way into kitchen garden or potato patch.

Soon we have partaken of a hasty but substantial breakfast, bountifully spread on the white tablecloth. Our bill is paid, and we make our way to the dock where lies the little steamer puffing and blowing, and straining at her fastenings, for though still tied to the wharf, her screw slowly churns the limpid water, the engine having been set in motion to prove whether the machinery is in proper working order. We are greeted with a kindly grasp of the hand by the jolly captain, who is perambulating the dock enjoying his morning pipe. The hands are busily engaged in taking in her cargo; our few traps are soon on board, and the canoes laid on the big punt invariably towed behind, the vessel being too small to admit of the necessary boats being carried on deck.

A toot from the whistle; the captain grasps the spokes of the wheel, gives a sharp pull to an adjacent wire; there is a loud tinkle of a bell in the engine room, a quick trembling motion and low rumbling noise. The dock, with its half dozen villagers who have come down to see us off, is quickly left behind as the plucky little vessel stems the placid waters at a speed of not less than eight miles an hour. Gracefully and swiftly she makes her way round the sharp bends of the river, past comfortable and thrifty homesteads, when gradually Lake of Bays opens to the view. The field glass is unslung from the shoulder, the focus adjusted, and seated in front of the wheelhouse, we gaze upon the varied beauties. Immediately in front, the lake is dotted here and there with high, rocky, pine-clad islands; every rock, tree, and limb is faithfully mirrored in the surrounding water—the shadow almost as distinct as the substance. There on the one hand are three or four loons, the great northern divers, with their beautiful plumage, each, like the islands, seemingly double. On the other side, the canoe of a settler swiftly approaches. A hat is waved; the whistle screams in answer. The engine room bell tinkles, the rumbling of the machinery and churning of the screw ceases, and we come to a standstill. The canoe delivers its message, and we are again away on our course.

A little farther on, wheeling to the shore, we tie up at a primitive wharf composed of a rough wooden pier with three or four logs extending from it to the shore and covered with a few loose planks. Piled on the bank are several cords of dry wood, a portion of which is speedily transferred to our hold, and the little vessel again ploughs her way through the calm waters of the lake.

The most of the south shore, as far as can be seen to the east, has been redeemed from the primeval forest, and where only a few years ago was an unbroken wilderness, there are now thriving and well-stocked farms with good dwellings and capacious barns. Right in front is a long, low, rocky point, the lake extending on its right some ten or twelve miles eastwards to the village of Colebridge [Dorset] at Cedar Narrows, famous for its trout, venison, and steaks of bear meat. Should the traveller wish to visit Hollow Lake, that is his route; but as we are bent for the headwaters of the branch of the Muskoka River that extends farther to the east, we steer to the north of the point, and a sheet of water larger than what we have yet seen opens to our sight.

The western shore is high and bluffy, the timber chiefly hardwood, while at short intervals the forest is broken by large clearings, well-fenced and cultivated, everything denoting the success and approaching independence of the hardy backwoodsman who only a few years ago penetrated these wilds, with in many cases only his axe and his hands, to hew out for himself a home in the unbroken and then almost unknown wilderness. How much this

Canada of ours owes to those hardy pioneers! What an evidence of the success that almost invariably attends the industrious and persevering! How is it that our towns and cities are so crowded with the poor and starving, with their cry of no work? Out here there are thousands of farm lots of one hundred acres each, which can be had free for the taking, on almost any of which many a labourer or artisan would be better off than in town or city. Here they have no rent, no high taxes, no water and gas rates, no high-priced fuel. On nearly the worst of the land they can grow at least potatoes and other vegetables, and keep their cow, pig, and hens, the three sources from which so many of the necessaries of life are drawn, while nearly all the year round abundance of work may be had at a good remuneration for any time that can be spared from the farm, and within a reasonable distance of their homes.

After steaming for over an hour we round another rocky point and are in sight of the end of our steamboating. Away in the distance we see through the glass the end of the north bay. A narrow strip of yellow sand lines the shore. Behind is a clearing filled with blackened and charred stumps, while in the front, a few rods up a gentle incline from the water's edge, stands a substantial frame house. At a distance of a mile and a quarter from the landing we pass a bold high bluff to our left. Right in our front, and an eighth of a mile from the landing, a large creek, the outlet of some two or three small lakes, pours its waters into the bay; while to the right, in a little recess, may be seen the mouth of the North River, the stream that we purpose ascending.

Another shrill scream from the whistle, a few more turns of the screw, another tinkle of the bell in the engine room, and the machinery stops. With lessening speed we approach and finally stop alongside the primitive dock of rough undressed logs. We have reached the village of Dwight at the head of the north bay, and the end of the first stage of our journey.

Stepping on shore, we are accorded a hearty greeting by the landlord of the Dwight Temperance House, and by a number of the hardy and bronzed settlers who have come out to get their weekly mail and make a few purchases at the little store, which, as well as the post office, is kept in conjunction with the Temperance House. Our goods are quickly transferred to shore, the mailbag changed, a few packages of merchandise, bags of flour, and sides of bacon laid out on the dock. After a hearty shake of the hand and a "bon voyage" from captain and engineer, the whole crew, the engine is again put in motion, and after backing off a few boat lengths, the signal is given, "full steam ahead." Wheeling round to the left, first her broadside, then the gracefully rounded stern and the turmoil of waters are presented to view. The little steamer proceeds on her way down round the peninsula that divides the north from the south bay, up which she progresses to Colebridge, when, after performing the same round of duties as at Dwight, the prow is again pointed westwards. When the rays of the setting sun illuminate the eastern hills, she again ties up at her dock of the morning, puffing and panting like a tired horse. The boat has made her daily round of the lake, and both vessel and crew have honestly earned their night's repose.

The view down the bay from the verandah of the Dwight House is a magnificent one. Across the bay to the right, the dense forest has given place to wide well-fenced fields of waving grain, with comfortable farmhouses and good barns. To the left, a similar transformation is taking place. Another opening in the woods down the left shore, and a wreath of curling blue smoke, denotes the presence of another of those elements of Ontario's greatness, the hardy pioneer. The remainder of the shore seen from this point of view is covered with a dense growth of maple, birch, and basswood, with an occasional gigantic pine or hemlock towering high above its fellows. Here and there a bold treeless bluff is visible at intervals between the trees, the rock nearly concealed by rich brown flower-besprinkled moss.

But in order to appreciate all the beauties of Lake of Bays, one must view it in the various seasons of the year. In winter, all is covered with a mantle of spotless white, the leafless boughs bent beneath the snow which is whirled at intervals by fierce northern blasts in dense white wreaths across the icebound waters. Soon as the warm rays of the spring sun have melted the snow and re-leased the water of the lake from its icy covering, the trees begin to unfold their buds, and in a few days all is in full summer dress of deep green; and the drumming of the partridge, the coo of the pigeon, and whistle of the robin are heard on every side. Again, as the warm summer draws to a close, the leaves begin to ripen, the frosty nights of October assisting Nature in her handiwork: first the maple shows a yellowish tinge, gradually deepening into var-ious shades of red; then the birch, beech, and lastly the basswood follow suit. Here, scenes of beauty that would task the powers of the most gifted pen or pencil are spread before the admiring eye.

Dwight has become of late years a favourite resort for the tourist, the lover of piscatorial sport, and the deer hunter. Many a huge trout has been hauled out of the deep waters of the bay, and many a noble buck received its death wound while breasting the foam-crested wave to escape the baying hound, which has roused him at early morn from his lair under the "greenwood tree." Here also, the overworked and confined city clerk can spend his brief summer holiday, and recruit his shattered nerves, inhaling the pure air of forest and lake; while he can sleep on a soft bed and sit down to a board loaded with nearly all the luxuries of the city, attended by the courteous landlady who seems bent only on ful-filling the most minute wants of her guests.

But now we are for the first time to partake of our own frugal fare. The tin tea pail and drinking dishes are unpacked, a fire is started by the side of a stump, the tea chest is opened, and half a handful of the fragrant leaves thrown into the pail of cold water—for experience has taught us that the best method of extracting all the nourishment is to put them into cold water, and remove the pail from the fire as soon as it has attained the boiling point. A small pole is procured and the tea pail hung on one end over the fire. The other end is thrust under a neighbouring log, with a billet of wood to support it in the middle. The frying pan, after being carefully cleaned, is filled also with water. An opening is made in the end of the rough canvas bag in which is the huge side of long clear bacon. The cook, knife in hand, is at work cutting off a number of slices, which are placed in the pan, set on the fire, and allowed to boil a couple of minutes. Called parboiling, this is to remove the superfluous salt. The water is now poured off, and the next moment the air is impregnated with the aroma of frying pork, which in a few minutes is cooked.

Suddenly there is a frizzing sound on the fire as a portion of the now boiling tea forces its way by the accumulating steam out round the sides of the lid. It is quickly removed from the fire, the lid taken off, and half a dishful of cold water thrown in, when the leaves immediately subside to the bottom. The head is knocked out of the biscuit barrel. The shout of the single word, "Dinner!" speedily brings all hands, each with tin plate and tea dish to the spot; when each, having helped himself to a slice of pork, a spoonful or two of gravy, and filled his dish with the fragrant tea, makes his way to the biscuit barrel, where a few of the hard brown discs are laid on top of the pork. A neighbouring log or spot of grass serves for a seat, the knees for a table, and do we enjoy the dinner? To use a homely and perhaps a rather vulgar phrase, "You bet!"

As this is the last chance of availing ourselves of Her Majesty's mail, while our cook washes the dishes and packs up, we hastily scribble a few lines to home and loved ones.

48

CHAPTER 3 NOTES    *From the head of navigation on Lake of Bays at Dwight, the Dickson party heads east into the wilderness along a crude wagon road—an ancestor of Highway 60—that bypasses the Oxtongue Rapids, a stretch of bouldery rapids and rocky chutes obstructing nearly 5 kilometres of the lower Oxtongue (North) River. At the foot of navigable waters above the main rapids, the party makes its first camp (this is a few hundred metres upstream from the bridge in Oxtongue Rapids Park). Luckily for early travellers, the Oxtongue Rapids is an anomaly: for most of its 48 kilometres the Oxtongue mainstream flows placidly, its 100-metre descent off the Algonquin highlands otherwise largely concentrated in falls requiring only modest portages.*

*Extensive stands of pine once covered the level sand plain east of Dwight; lumbermen cut timber here in the 1870s, but had gone no farther up the Oxtongue when Dickson travelled through the area. Tree note: the black birch on page 50 is yellow birch, a common species in the hardwood forests of the region. The bark on older trees is quite dark.*

*Dickson mentions the sad case of Isaac Hunter, pioneer recluse and possible fugitive from the 1837 Rebellion, who in the 1860s homesteaded on the Oxtongue at the end of the Bobcaygeon Road. The location at the above-noted bridge is still called Hunter's Bridge—this is on the surveyed road line—but in rare confusion Dickson's account infers that the original bridge crossed farther downstream. The road was never much more than a trail north of Dorset (which, incidentally, got its name in 1883; Dickson still uses the old names, Cedar Narrows and Colebridge.)*

*The modern canoe tripper, outfitted with nylon tent, shock-corded fibreglass poles, freeze-dried beef stroganoff, and one-burner backpacking stove, should get a kick out of Dickson's account of the domestic side of wilderness travel in the 1880s—definitely not lightweight or low-impact tripping! The food and cooking techniques are those of the "working" explorer and bush camp of the era.*

*The problem of bedfellows who won't stay on their own side in the confined quarters of a tent has never been solved.*

## 3

## *First Night in Camp*

————

THE NORTH RIVER FOR THE FIRST EIGHT OR TEN MILES ABOVE LAKE of Bays, with the exception of the first two, is composed of a series of roaring chutes and rapids, too rough for canoeing. What is a chute? It is a short stretch where there is not a perpendicular fall, but the stream, hemmed in and somewhat narrowed in its channel by projecting rocks, dashes foaming and tossing down an inclined plane over sharp-pointed rocks and large boulders, terminating at the bottom in either a deep bay or a rapid. We must take our things overland five miles to a point half a mile above Hunter's Bridge, the distance by the winding stream being nearly twice as far. The services of a settler and his team are secured, and a couple of men are sent on ahead with axes to cut any newly fallen trees out of the way.

The goods are loaded on the wagon; the canoes, if taken on the load, would run a fair chance of being broken on the rough road, so they must be carried. They are laid bottom-down upon the ground, and two paddles laid along the two centre thwarts and fastened thereto, a sufficient distance apart to allow the head of the bearer to pass up between. Then, stooping and grasping a gunwale with each hand, we carefully raise the one end, turn her over above the head, and let her down till a paddle rests on either shoulder, the other end still resting on the ground; then, slightly stooping, we bend forward till the light vessel is neatly balanced on the shoulders, and now, straightening up, the hands still grasping the gunwales, away we march in single file after the wagon.

For the first three miles the country is level, with a ridge of hardwood hills at a short distance from the road on the north. The axe of the lumberman and the ravages of the fire-king have well-nigh destroyed all the original forest between the hill to the north and the river on the south. It has been succeeded by a growth of white birch, poplar, and red cherry, the whole surface being covered by wild raspberry and black thimbleberry. Twining amongst the roots, the slender vines of the still more luscious strawberry are in equal abundance, while here and there are clumps of black alder and the sumac with its big clusters of small red fruit.

We pass through a few small abandoned clearings. A small lake [Spring] lies nestled in its margin of marsh grass in a hollow to the left, while the roar of the river tumbling over its rocky bed may be heard at short intervals on the right. The hardwood hill to the north now bends southerly across our path, and we cross a few ridges covered with a dense growth of huge maples, black birch, and hemlock. A mile or so farther we come to a stop on top of a hill some three hundred feet high, down which the road is cut in an almost straight line. Here, far down in the hollow, we catch glimpses of the silvery river shining through the trees, running at right angles to our path and spanned by a little dilapidated bridge. This is Hunter's Bridge, and is as far as the road has been built.

On the edge of the hill, on the farther bank of the stream, is an old deserted clearing an acre or two in extent, with the remains of a shanty in the centre. Here, a number of years ago, a man named Hunter built his cabin and moved his family into the woods far from any other settler. He was in the habit of crossing the country at regular intervals to the settlement of Cedar Narrows some nine miles to the south. During the depths of an uncommonly severe winter a longer interval than usual elapsed since his last visit, and the settlers at the Narrows became alarmed for his safety. Mr. C [Zack Cole], with the never-failing solicitude that one dweller in the bush feels for the welfare of another, donned his snowshoes and alone made the long tramp over the deep soft snow. The poor man was found laid out a corpse in his lonely hut. He had been dead for several days. The mateless woman and fatherless children huddled round a small fire eating a few frozen potatoes, their only food. The breadwinner was gone.

Hunter's Bridge is the eastern terminus of a government colonization road, and connects also at this point with the northern terminus of the Bobcaygeon Road. We now turn to the left, and the wagon proceeds half a mile farther over a rough trail, when it reaches the end of its journey. At noon we bade goodbye to steam power; now we must part with horse and wagon. Henceforth our only means of transport will be the bark canoe along the smooth stretches of river and across the lakes, while crossing the portages, bending beneath our packs with tumpline across the brow, we must be our own pack mules. The wagon is quickly unloaded, turned round with some difficulty amongst the closely growing trees, and is away on its homeward journey. Here our labour begins in earnest. Hastily turning the canoes bottom upwards, for the gradually gathering clouds portend an approaching shower, as many of the goods as they will cover are placed underneath; as much of the remainder as we will be unable to take in the first trip is piled together and covered with a light rubber sheet. Each man now hastily snatching up a pack and swinging it upon the shoulder, we hurry off along the narrow trail. One hand grasps the tumpline, while with the other we ward off the numerous limbs projecting across the path, which if not thus guarded against might play sad havoc with eye and face. We scramble, or half roll, over a fallen tree or two, and bend beneath another that has been torn out by the roots by some passing storm and arrested in its fall by coming in contact with another. Another half mile and again the shining river, glinting through the trees, bursts upon the view. A few steps more and we reach the landing. Only a very small piece of the stream is visible from this point, while to the right we hear the roar of a short rapid where the river is divided into two parts by a small island at the top of a rock ledge. We have reached our first campground.

Tossing the packs off, we seat ourselves for a moment upon them, while hats are removed and pocket handkerchiefs hastily applied to reddened brows and perspiring faces. We straighten up and gaze for a few minutes on a scene of sylvan beauty. The view is very limited in extent, for neither fire nor the lumberman has caused destruction here, and great pines, maple, hemlock, and cedar, with a dense undergrowth of balsam and hazel, encircle us on every side. But there is little time for either rest or meditation, for though the clouds are passing off without the threatened shower, the slanting rays of the fast-declining sun denote the near approach of night. The remainder of the goods are to be brought in from the end of the road. Tents must be put up, brush for the beds cut, gathered, and spread, and firewood for the night procured—for though here in abundance and to spare, it still must be cut and brought in. Then the fire must be started, packs undone, supper cooked and eaten, and a dozen and one other odd jobs, known only to those accustomed to a life in the woods, to be got through with before darkness finally sets in.

The campground is an old one, used for many years by surveyors, hunters, and trappers, so there is no clearing off or levelling of ground to be done. The force is divided. A part returns for the remainder of the baggage, while two others cut tent poles and pegs, and set up the tent. Another cuts down a balsam, carefully selecting one with a large top. The pin-covered limbs are broken off a short distance from the trunk, and brought in. The tent has been erected, carefully and evenly stretched, and the brushing is begun. We commence at the back by laying down each separate limb with its top to the rear and the side that was undermost on the tree turned on top. We continue this process till the whole surface is covered with a sufficient thickness to make a soft and even bed, care being taken to keep the broken ends next to the ground. A pole, five or six inches in diameter, is laid across the ends of the brush at the door, and kept in its place by pegs driven into the ground at each end. The whole floor now presents a soft, smooth, dark green elastic surface.

By this time the goods are all in except the canoes, and as neither bears nor wolves will eat them, and there are no thieves here, they are safe where they are. A few projecting limbs have been left four or five inches long on the upright pole at the back of the tent, on which to hang powder horn, shot bag, field glass, etc., while the rifle and double-barrel are stacked round, carefully tied to the same pole, for the double purpose of protecting them from the damp and reducing the chances of an accident to a minimum. The packs are opened, and our dunnage bags and everything not immediately wanted stored away in the bole at the back of the tent. The blankets are spread out and rolled back to the head till bedtime. Our heavy boots are removed and replaced by light and easy pairs of gaiters or moccasin slippers. We begin to feel at home and are quite comfortable.

Darkness has now set in, and what about supper? Our cook has not been idle. A huge fire blazes a few feet in front of the door. A stout post about four feet long has been securely driven into the ground a foot or so from each end of the fire. Each is cut from the top of a small tree where the trunk branched off into two parts, the branches being lopped off a few inches above the point of divergence, thus forming a crotch. Across these another stout pole has been laid, from which the tea pail depends. The cold water and dry leaves are in process of quick transformation into tea.

The cook, with glowing but merry face, leans over the frying pan, carefully stirring up and turning the frizzling slices of the "unclean beast." The little can of mustard is got out; the one bottle of pickles is produced, and the neck broken off to save the trouble of drawing the cork. In a few minutes everything is ready, and the dinner scene is enacted over again. Pork and biscuits and dishes of tea disappear with amazing quickness and in goodly quantities, for the afternoon's work has given all hands a good appetite, while joke and jest are bandied from side to side.

Supper finished, pocketknives, pipes, and plugs of T.B. or Myrtle Navy are produced. We have no tobacco pouches with ready-cut, but prefer cutting a pipeful as it is required. Pipes are lit and a general smoke begun. The sight is a pleasing one. Here one sits on the ground, back against a log, puffing away in silence; two or three, seated on the pole at the door of the tent, engage in quiet conversation, discussing the morrow's programme; others recline on elbow or stretch at full length on the dry leaves. One who does not indulge in the weed lies with hands under head on the brush in the tent, singing in a lusty voice.

We retire a few paces into the shade and survey the scene. We have seen on canvas many pictures of camp life, but never aught that did the scene justice. The merry group and the white tent; the blazing fire and illuminated trunks of the huge pines; the lights and shadows amongst the green leaves, and the silvery ripple of the river where a single ray from the fire penetrates to its surface; the glittering stars overhead and the soft mellow light of the moon as she shows her face above the eastern hill; the solemn stillness of the night, broken only by the gentle murmur of the adjacent rapid ... attempt to describe it. Pshaw!

The cook is hard at work. The dishes have been washed and

carefully piled, bottom-up, on a piece of newly peeled hemlock bark. All the birch within a considerable radius of this old camp-ground has long since been denuded of its yellow coat. Pork is to be parboiled for breakfast, and more boiled for dinner. The round-pointed steel shovel has had a handle inserted in its socket. A hole a foot and a half in diameter, and of an equal depth, has been dug close to the fire and filled with burning embers to dry out and heat it. A tin pail half filled with water is got ready. The bag of white beans is brought forth, a few tea-dishfuls are carefully picked over and emptied into the pail of water, which is now hung over the fire. Another pail of water is placed alongside it. The sack of dried apples is brought within the radius of the light, a few handfuls taken out and carefully washed in the big tin dish, then squeezed between the hands and dropped into the second pail. The dirty water is now thrown out of the dish, and replaced by a few dipperfuls of clean hot water. The sack of bacon is again visited. Several square chunks are cut off, tossed into the dish of hot water, scraped and washed clean, and deposited in still another pail of water, which takes its place as number three over the fire.

Our cook has now a breathing spell, and time to light his pipe also and join in the conversation for half an hour or so. At the end of that time the lid of the apple pail is removed, a large iron fork is thrust down to the bottom, and the whole mass stirred up. Another dipper of water is added, as the swelling fruit has ab-sorbed most of the first supply. The lid is then replaced, and the bean pot treated in a similar manner. The pail of boiling pork is also subjected to a careful scrutiny to ascertain if it is not boiling dry. A part of the top is now taken off a box of raisins, from which a few handfuls are carefully picked and washed clean. Another inspection of the apple pail shows that the cooking has reached the proper stage; it is removed from the fire, the raisins are emp-tied in and carefully and evenly mixed with the apples, when the pail is again replaced on the fire and allowed to simmer for a few minutes. Finally it is taken off, a few spoonfuls of sugar are added, the lid is replaced, and it is set to one side ready for breakfast.

A bake kettle hitherto kept in the background now makes its appearance, and is scraped and thoroughly cleaned. The beans, which are by this time boiled soft, are emptied into it along with the grease from the pork we had for supper. A few slices of raw fat pork are laid on top and the lid is put on. The hole by the fire is emptied of its embers, a quantity of hot sand thrown in, and the bake kettle put in on top, the whole being covered with hot sand and ashes. The boiling pork is now also done to a turn; it is taken from the fire, the swollen pieces held up in turn on the prongs of the big fork, and cold water poured over them, when it also is set aside ready for the table. The cook's work is now over for the day, or rather the night, for we hear his "Get out of the way, boys; I want to go to bed."

It is now time for all hands to retire, for we must be astir betimes in the morning. The slight preparations for turning in are soon made. The wide-brimmed straw hat is placed bottom-up a little above where the head is intended to rest. The contents of the trousers pockets are emptied into the crown. No small article must be left round in a loose manner, or the chances are that it will be lost in the brush. The vest is folded, watch pocket uppermost, and laid on top of the hat. Braces and socks are removed and placed under the dunnage bag, which, along with coat or smockfrock, will form our pillow. The blankets have been unrolled, and turning down the upper end of one of them, we slide in between.

"Are you coming to bed, Jack?" is addressed to a smoker seated at the door, reluctant to abandon the fragrant weed.

"Yes, just in a minute, Tom."

"Well, you'd better hurry up then, and not disturb a fellow when he's asleep."

"Lie over, Jim, and straighten one of those big legs of yours, and try to be satisfied with your own half of the bed."

"Now, Dick, straighten yourself out; I'm quite willing to let you have half the bed, but must protest against your taking it out of the middle."

"Straighten yourself, Bob, and keep your big feet to your own side"—accompanied by a preliminary snore.

Such are a few of the expressions, garnished by sundry adjectives not necessary, nor polite, to repeat, that are heard on every side. A hushed conversation is still being carried on by one or two couples, when, "Come now, boys, you had better adjourn the debate till morning," is heard from the boss. This gentle and easily understood reminder is at once taken, and in few minutes all is hushed in silence broken only by the heavy breathing of the sleepers and the gentle murmur of the flowing river.

The first rays of the rising sun are just beginning to change the green tops of the giant pines into golden when a loud "Hurrah, boys, breakfast; are you going to sleep all day?" is heard from the cook, who has been up since the first grey streak of dawn. In an incredibly short space of time all are up. The few articles of clothing taken off the previous evening are donned, while negative compliments touching the respective merits as bedfellows are bandied from side to side, accompanied by a gentle reminder to the one who had spread the brush of "a big root or limb, right under my back or shoulder," and the ready and consoling retort, "If you don't like my work, you can make it yourself tonight"; all, however, in the best of humour.

Towel, soap, and comb in hand, we make our way to the side of the river. We have frequently read descriptions of the morning ablutions of camp life, in which the campers are represented as standing on stone or log and stooping down to bathe the head in the water. This method we consider inconvenient and awkward, so we have provided ourselves with a handy tin wash dish, which we fill with water and set on a moss-covered log or neighbouring bank at a convenient height from the ground to avoid an unnecessary amount of stooping. After scrubbing hands, face, and neck, the dish is emptied and immediately taken possession of by the next in waiting. The hasty toilet soon completed, we wend our way back to camp.

The pail of hot tea and pan of fried pork stand invitingly ready. The shovel is again called into play to scrape the ashes off the top of the buried bake kettle. A hook, cut from an adjacent sapling, is inserted into each ear; the kettle is gently lifted out and set down at a convenient distance from the fire. The dust is carefully wiped off the lid, one of the hooks inserted in the ring on top, and the lid is lifted off, exposing the rich steaming mess to our admiring gaze. Spoons are at once dipped in; each one helps himself, a liberal quantity being laid on each plate. The biscuit barrel is again relieved of a portion of its contents, and with light hearts and hungry stomachs we find seats and begin the wholesome repast. In a few minutes both pork and beans have vanished. The plates are replenished with a few spoonfuls of the apple sauce we so carefully prepared the preceding evening.

In fifteen or twenty minutes the meal is over, for when we sit down to eat here, we mean business, and very little conversation is indulged in, except for a few stray remarks—

"That's what will stick to a fellow's ribs, boys!"

"Is that your fifth biscuit, Charlie?"

"It is none of your (adjective) business, Bill."

"Better set down your plate and take the pot, Chris"—the speaker being in doubt whether the said plate or the pot contains the most beans.

Breakfast over and pipes lit, we must now begin to pack up and prepare for the start up the river.

CHAPTER 4 NOTES   *Finally—the canoes go in the water and the expedition up the Oxtongue River begins in earnest. The section of the river traversed in this chapter, a quiet reach rarely used by canoeists today, extends only 2 kilometres up to the heavy rapids at the outlet of Oxtongue Lake; much of the narrative is given over to provisioning, packing, and canoeing advice for the novice traveller. Dickson uses the fragile birchbark canoe, workhorse of Indians and explorers for centuries, even though sturdier canvas-covered canoes were readily available by the 1880s. Light, cheap, highly manoeuverable, and easily repaired, the bark craft remained the preference of many woodsmen.*

*Dickson scoffs at the prodigious quantity of supplies the "amateur" adventurer takes into the wilds, but the amount his own party packs would certainly boggle today's tripper. You don't see many 100-pound sacks of salt pork getting lugged over portages now! Omitted today too is the "ague" medicine—quinine-laced brandy (at least, the quinine is omitted). Ague, or malaria, is a tropical disease, although the term was often used for any mysterious fever. The mere thought of having to drink the bitter home-made medicine would likely cure anybody of anything.*

*Part of Dickson's directions to make a pack with tumpline has been reconstructed, as the original was even harder to follow. Essentially, the pack consisted of goods rolled up in blankets and securely bound with leather straps, one strap projecting in a loop that hung on the forehead of the bearer. For portaging heavy loads short distances, the system worked well, but modern pack designs are considerably more comfortable.*

*Knee-high leather boots are certainly not the preferred footwear for canoeing today. The image evoked by Dickson's description of the men standing around emptying them of water is a hilarious one.*

*Dickson of course uses miles and feet for distances, but also the less common rod (16½ feet, or 5 metres) and the chain (66 feet, or about 20 metres). The latter is a surveyor's measure.*

*Incidentally, when Dickson says "we" or "our," he sometimes means the whole party, sometimes himself and canoe partner, often just himself.*

# 4

## *A Canoe Voyage*

THE CANOES ARE SENT FOR AND SOON LAID ALONGSIDE A LOG THAT extends out into the water of the little eddy. The ends are drawn a foot or two onto the soft shore to prevent their floating away. The tent is struck, and we proceed to arrange our goods and make the packs. We have been careful not to overstock ourselves with a superabundance of either clothing or provisions. It is a source of no small amusement to the genuine woodman to witness the vast quantity of supplies the amateur feels it necessary to take with him for a few days, or at most, weeks, sojourn in the bush: the heavy canvas tent with extra projecting fly; the bundles of blankets, waterproofs, rubber sheets, and inflatable India-rubber bed and pillow; the boxes of bread, biscuit, and cheese; the bottles of pickles and spices; the cans of condensed milk and prepared fruits; the rolls of spiced bacon and tins of fresh beef and pressed vegetables; and last, but by no means least, the demijohns of gin and brandy, bottles of old rye, and boxes of cigars.

They have been in the enjoyment of nearly all the luxuries of a city larder, all the comforts of the drawing room, and after a sojourn of a week or two, return to town and recount to sympathizing groups the many hardships they have endured. They tell of the many hours of severe toil, seated in the bow of a canoe holding the end of a trawling line and puffing a Havana while a hired assistant paddled them round; or, with rifle in hand, borne swiftly across the lake propelled by the strong arms of the guide in pursuit of an unfortunate deer driven in by the hounds; or standing by the foot of a fall or rapid, casting the fly to tempt the speckled denizens of the waters, with a dozen mosquitoes and half as many black flies and sandflies buzzing round vainly endeavouring to effect an entrance to gloved hand or veil-protected face and neck. They have endured all those hardships, and now return home vainly hugging the idea they have been "roughing it."

Let us inspect our larder. There are several sides of long clear bacon, Ramsey's best, sewn up in coarse brown canvas bags, about one hundred pounds in each sack. We have several bags of the best flour, and a barrel of biscuits sufficient to last till we can be long enough in one camp to enable the cook to bake loaf bread; a box of mixed green and black tea; a sack of dried applies; a few bushels of white beans—the smaller the bean the better the quality; a quantity of split peas for soup; a box or two of raisins; a quantity of rice and sugar; and a few bars of the best soap—a sufficient proportion of each to last the time we purpose being out. Each man carries his own tobacco. A few small cans each of mustard and pepper, a bag of table salt, a box of matches, and pound or two of yeast cakes and baking soda are in the immediate charge of the cook. This is our larder. For liquors we have none, except for a half-gallon tin flask filled with the best brandy, into which, by advice of our family physician, we have put a sufficient quantity of quinine to make it a valuable ague medicine, should we be threatened with an attack of that enervating and troublesome disease.

For protection against the weather we have one large tent of No. 3 duck or heavy twilled grey cotton for ourselves and men, and another smaller one to hold the cookery and provisions. Each man has one pair of the largest and best grey blankets, and by way of wearing apparel, a pair of strong kip or cowhide boots, with patch bottoms and Hungarian tacks in the soles—the leg must not be long enough to interfere with the free use of the knee joint; a pair of light gaiters, or moccasins or leather slippers, to put on when round camp; three or four pairs of light woollen socks; a couple of pairs of strong guernsey drawers and as many shirts of the same material, and two strong cotton ones; one pair of brown duck and another pair of woollen pants; one coat and vest; a few coloured cotton handkerchiefs; and a hat and towel. This comprises the whole of our wardrobe. Experience has taught us that it is a sufficient supply for all our wants. What is not required for immediate use we stow away in a common cotton grain bag, the whole weighting only a few pounds, known as the dunnage bag.

The writer of this has lived in the woods under canvas for months at a time, and at all seasons of the year, and has found the above-mentioned supplies ample; but if it is to be a winter party, the clothing will require to be of heavier material, with the addition of mitts and moccasins, and in deep snow, snowshoes will also be necessary. He has invariably brought his men out healthy, fat, wiry, and strong, and fitted for any amount of hard work.

But we must get to work and pack up. A pair of blankets is spread and doubled on the ground, and the tumpline laid upon them. The tumpline is made of three leather straps. Two of them are about six feet long by three-fourths of an inch wide, one end tapering to a point, and three inches of the other passing through and securely sewn to a small iron ring. These are laid parallel across the blankets about two and one-half feet apart. The other strap, of good stiff harness leather, is two feet long by three inches wide at the middle, with tapered ends that have been sewn to the iron rings on the long straps, connecting those two, the broad part projecting beyond the edge of the blankets. The ends of the blankets are then turned in over the longer straps. Some other neatly folded blankets, dunnage bags, and other small traps—a sufficient quantity to make up the pack—are laid thereon. One man now seizes the broad part, or head band, near the iron rings. Another takes hold of the end of the straps at the edge of the blankets on the opposite side. Each raises up his side, and the ends of the long thongs are passed through the rings. Then, each man straightening himself up, thong in hand and a foot pressed on the pack, pulls them tight. A half knot then being made at each ring, the ends of the blankets are drawn together till they overlap. The thongs are crossed in the middle, the men changing with each other, and again drawn tight. The pack is now turned over and the thongs that have been passed round it again change hands. A half knot is made and the pulling process is repeated till it will yield no more. A double knot is now made.

The pack, now completed, is nearly round. The broad part of the line forms a big loop, and to raise the pack up, this is seized by the hands close to the rings, and by one swinging lift the pack is landed on the shoulders with the broad part across the forehead. If it has been properly made it will be small in comparison to its weight, will stand any amount of knocking round without becoming undone, and can be easily stowed away in the canoe. All the remainder of the goods are done up in like manner.

The bake kettle is carefully done up in one of the tents to prevent it from being accidentally broken. In the meantime, the cook has got his dishes washed, and is stowing them away also so as to make the least possible bulk. The tea pail, which is usually the smallest, is selected. Our cooking utensils have been all made to order, so there is little difficulty in putting them together. First, the tin plates are laid in the bottom; next, the tea dishes are put in; the spoons, knives, and forks follow, all having been carefully counted to see that none are lost. The lid is put on, the pail set in the next largest, the handle turned down, and the lid of this one also put in its place; and the same process is gone through with till the largest alone is visible. The lid of this latter one is now securely tied on, a tumpline wound round the whole and tied with the projecting loop to receive the forehead of the carrier. Everything is now ready, and we proceed to load the canoes.

But while that is being done, another small but important matter must be attended to. Our birchen canoes are frail craft, easily damaged. A scrape on a stone, or bump against a snag, may pierce a hole in the bottom, or at least knock off a small piece of the gum from its seams, which are sewn together with the pliant roots of the tamarack—the watap [thread] of the Indians—and then coated over with gum. A small leak soaking into the cedar lining, thereby adding materially to its weight, besides wetting the goods, would quickly be the result. In order to be always prepared for such an emergency, each one is provided with a "gum dish." A quantity of unmade shoemaker's resin, or tamarack gum, to which sufficient grease to overcome its brittleness is added, is put in the dish and placed on the fire till the whole is thoroughly melted and mixed together. It is then taken off and allowed to cool. Whenever a leak begins to show, the canoe is at once run on shore, emptied of its load, and turned bottom-up. A small fire is made, and the gum dish placed thereon in charge of an attendant. The bottom and ends of the little craft are carefully examined; if no hole is visible, the lips are now applied successively to certain suspicious-looking spots, pressed tight to the bark, and the breath sucked in. If we can draw in air, the leak has been found. A small wooden spoon, hastily made with a pocketknife, is dipped in the melted resin, a small portion neatly spread over the hole, and the leak stopped. The tiny craft is then replaced in the water and held in place by one of the crew so that no part touches either a stone or the shore, while the other replaces the load, and again seating in their places, they paddle away on their course. The whole delay is not more than ten or fifteen minutes.

Our canoes are now loaded. Each pack is laid gently in its place, in such a manner as to leave the bow a few inches higher than the stern. A sufficient space is left in both bow and stern for the two men who form the crew. The bowman takes his place, kneeling on the bottom, his knees resting on a few balsam or cedar boughs. The steersman, with paddle in hand, gently shoves her a few feet out into deeper water; then, as the other steadies her with the blade of his paddle resting on the surface of the water, he steps lightly in, also kneeling on newly plucked boughs. The canoe is then shoved out a few lengths and turned broadside to the shore. Resting on their paddles, they now ask, "How is she trimmed, boys?" and the answer is given, "All right." The paddles, one on the right, the other on the left, are now dipped in the water at the same moment, and propelled by the powerful strokes of strong arms, the little fairy shoots swiftly and gracefully forward on her course. In a few minutes the others are loaded. The boss or cook takes a careful look round to see that nothing has been forgotten, and we are off.

The shores of the river here are completely overhung by projecting cedars, alder, birch, and hemlock, with here and there the top of a fallen tree nodding and swaying, the lower limbs being submerged in the rippling water; while straight tapering cedars, denuded of their limbs but studded with sharp projecting knots, lie treacherously a few inches underneath the surface. It is the duty of the man in the bow to be constantly on the lookout for those hidden dangers, for a moment's carelessness may be the cause of a hole being pierced in the bow of the frail bark, or a sudden capsize spilling both men and goods into the stream.

As we are now about entering a section of country that is the undisturbed home of the deer and moose, of the beaver and muskrat, the man of the party who is the best shot and has the quickest eye is selected for the bowman in the foremost canoe.

The loaded rifle, or double-barrel, one barrel loaded with ball, the other with No. 3 shot, is laid carefully, the butt between his knees and muzzle projecting upwards over the bow of the canoe, ready to be snatched up and fired at any moment. The occupants of the first canoe are instructed to keep at least a quarter mile in advance of the rest of the party.

At the distance of only a few chains above the starting point there is a short rapid, and we must be careful to shoot the canoe in between a projecting cedar top on the left and some slightly submerged boulders on the right. Directly in front, little ripples on the water indicate the presence of other rocks that must also be avoided; but with a few swift skilful strokes of the paddles we are into the smooth waters above, the water curling up round the bow and gliding to tiny bubbles past the sides of the slim vessel.

At the end of a five-minute paddle, a low murmuring sound ahead denotes our approach to another rapid. There is a bend in the stream, and a few rods ahead some tufts of tall grass, sur-rounded by smooth, dark, water-worn shingle, are seen on the left. The river rushes down in tiny wavelets over its stony bed on the right. We paddle gently up the right shore, assisted in our progress by the little eddy invariably found at the foot of every rapid. Now the paddling ceases altogether, and we glide slowly forward till a slight grating noise is heard underneath. The canoe has touched the bottom, and we are at a standstill. The steersman presses his paddle tightly on the bottom, the paddle and gunwale grasped firmly with one hand to hold the canoe steadily in place, while the bowman, laying his paddle across the gunwale in front of him, rises slowly to his feet and steps lightly out into the water, firmly grasping the bow with his right hand at the same time. Here there is no waiting for orders; each knows the part he is expected to perform, and is ready for it. He now pushes the bow gently out a little, so as to bring the stern into the shallow water in order that the steersman also may step out without incurring the risk of getting wet.

We can lead her up this rapid with her load, so, laying the paddles on top and taking hold, one at each end, we commence wading and guiding her up the stream. The slightest touch on the bottom is easily and distinctly felt. Suddenly she comes to a full stop; her bow has run upon a hidden stone or tree root. A single glance shows us where there is sufficient water to float her. She is gently backed down a foot or two. We step a little farther into the stream. We may get over the boot-tops or suddenly step into an unseen hole up to the waist, but what of that? The water is warm, and in anticipation of such an accident, matches, tobacco, and pipes have been stuck in the ribbon of our hats. In a few minutes we reach the head of the rapid, and our canoe lies safely by the side of the deep still water.

We stand still for a few minutes to allow the water to drip from our wet bodies, then leaning with one hand on our paddles, we raise one foot up behind, and taking hold of the toe of the boot, bend it up as far as we can, when the water pours out at the knee. A like performance with the other foot, and we get rid of as much of the water as has not been absorbed by our clothes.

We again embark and have another half-hour paddle along short stretches of almost still water, with occasional short, quick spurts where it rushes with accelerated speed round sharp bends. The stream is everywhere overhung with dark green cedar, hemlock, and balsam, and here and there a soft maple, birch, and clump of alder. Here a naked trunk, which numerous spring floods with their loads of ice have completely denuded of both limbs and bark, lays out far into the water only a few inches above the surface, with root still firmly held on shore. We observe a spot where a few chips have been knocked off the top, and a short hardwood peg driven into the yielding water-soaked timber a few inches from it. What does this mean? It is where a trapper has set his steel trap the previous fall or spring to catch the little muskrat, as he will most likely do again as soon as the close season is over, and the furred denizens of the forest have donned their winter garb of rich, glossy, frost-defying fur.

The small ring at the end of the chain to which the trap is attached is passed over the little peg. The trap, after the spring has been set, is laid on the spot from where the chip has been cut. During the night Master Rat is in the habit of making a roost of this log, for what particular purpose man knoweth not. He incautiously sets his little foot on the spring. A sharp click, a sudden spring and plunge into the water, and he hangs by the foot completely submerged. After a brief struggle a drowned rat dangles from the end of the chain. Next morning the trapper paddles up, takes the game out, and resets the trap for another victim. But how does he know on which log to set his trap? As the partridge invariably drums on the same fallen tree, so this denizen of the water returns to the same log, which is easily distinguished from its fellows by the quantity of excrement left thereon.

But while surveying the log and discussing the method of taking the muskrat, we have forgotten the distance we have come. We are now entering a little bay, with a sudden bend to the right at the head of it, and another and somewhat larger one opens on the view. On entering this bay the ears are greeted by the sudden noise of rushing waters. Looking up, we see, a little to the left and about ten chains distant, a mass of water tumbling out of a small opening amongst the trees.

A few more strokes of the paddle, and there the rest of our canoes lie at the head of the bay a short distance to the left. They have reached the landing at the foot of the first portage.

CHAPTER 5 NOTES   *Winds on even a modest lake can spell trouble for a birchbark canoe—as the Dickson party discovers on Oxtongue, the first lake encountered on the journey up the Oxtongue River.*

With its sand beaches and scenic wooded hills all around, Oxtongue Lake today is a popular cottage and resort area on Highway 60, which was extended through here and on up the Oxtongue valley to Algonquin Park in the 1930s. Even in the early 1880s, according to Dickson, the area was drawing tourists in the form of deer hunters. The only substantial sign of civilization then was the presence of two small pioneer homesteads on the west shore. Sand plains bordering the lake provided a pocket of tillable soil in the midst of this rugged countryside. In the late 1880s the lumbermen marched into the surrounding hills to begin cutting the pine. They soon constructed a dam at the outlet of the lake to store water to flush logs down the Oxtongue Rapids and on to Lake of Bays.

At the time Dickson writes about, there was apparently no road to Oxtongue Lake (the homesteaders probably had a trail running out to Hunter's Bridge). Not long afterwards, likely when lumbering began, the wagon road was extended east from Hunter's Bridge. When Dickson travelled to Algonquin Park with Chief Ranger Peter Thomson in 1893, a hired wagon transported the canoes and gear all the way from Dwight to Oxtongue Lake, bypassing the lower Oxtongue River entirely. The Gilmour lumber company's tote road from Dorset to the Oxtongue headwaters (completed later in 1893) and the Booth railway (fully operational in 1897) rendered the river obsolete as an access route to the highlands, but the section above Oxtongue Lake became popular with recreational canoeists. Today, most of the river remains in a natural state.

Oxtongue Lake was named in 1853 by geologist Alexander Murray on account of its shape. The river, then called the Muskoka, later the North (because it's the main northern tributary of Lake of Bays), didn't become known as the Oxtongue until the 1890s.

The fish hawk, or osprey (next page), is a large fish-eating raptor. The "grey Canada bird" on page 73 is likely the gray (Canada) jay.

# 5

## *Caught in a Thunderstorm*

————

THERE IS ONLY ROOM FOR ONE TO LAND AT A TIME. WHILE THE FIRST canoe unloads, the men quietly rest in the others. As soon as the contents of the first have been tossed on shore, that canoe is lifted out and placed bottom-up a few yards from shore to leave room for the others. We are quickly alongside.

"What did you shoot, boys?" We had heard a shot a few minutes after the first canoe left.

"Oh, it was only Jack firing at the fish-hawk nest on top of that tall pine stump, on the west shore a short distance above the first rapid."

"Did he hit it?"

"Well, he made the old lady leave and the young imps squeal."

In a few minutes everything is on shore. With stooping heads and laden shoulders we hike across the level portage of a quarter of a mile or so, to the foot of Ox-Tongue Lake. We are now in the township of McClintock, having crossed the boundary between it and Franklin a short distance above the starting point.

This being the first day of our canoeing, we had everything to arrange and were late in getting a start. For as every man has his own particular duty to perform, so every canoe has its own portion of the goods to carry, and by this arrangement the danger of anything being left behind or forgotten is reduced to a minimum.

By this time the sun has well-nigh reached the meridian: we conclude we had better have dinner before re-embarking. The pack of pails, henceforth termed the cookery, is taken over the first trip. While the cook unpacks, starts the fire, and sets the tea a-going, the balance of the stuff is got over. Wet socks and clothing are taken off and hung up in the bright sunshine to dry, others being substituted in their places.

"That biscuit barrel is awkward to carry," one says. "I don't mind the weight of the darned thing, but it cuts into a fellow's back so. Couldn't we put the biscuit in a bag and leave it here?"

As we can see no reasonable ground for opposing this, we give our consent. The top is once more and for the last time taken out, and while one holds a bag, two men speedily transfer the contents of the barrel. It takes two bags to hold the biscuits. Emptied, the maligned "birrel" is unceremoniously kicked to one side.

The tea is very soon ready, the boiled pork produced, when each one, a biscuit with a slice of pork in one hand, a dish of hot tea in the other, finds a seat in some shady nook to discuss the frugal but wholesome fare. Dinner is soon over, and while the cook washes the dishes, stows away the fragments, and packs up, the after-dinner pipe is indulged in. While we are in full enjoyment of the fragrant weed, the sun is suddenly obscured. A low rumbling noise is heard in the northwest. A sudden wind begins to moan in fitful gusts amongst the tree tops. In a few minutes a thunderstorm will be upon us. Instantly every man is on his feet, for all know what is required in such a case. Two, axe in hand, are off into the woods for tent poles, some more clear a sufficient space for the tent, another hastily cuts and points tent pins, while still others gather the clothes that had been hung up to dry, and stow a portion of the goods under the upturned canoes. In an incredibly short space of time the tent is up, everything made snug, and we watch the rapidly approaching storm.

In a few minutes it is upon us in all its fury. Dark masses of clouds, rent by vivid flashes of forked lightning, chase each other in rapid succession towards the southeast. Loud peals of thunder follow quickly one upon the other. The trees shake and bend in the fierce gale that now rages. Fragments of limbs are torn off the trees and borne far out on the lake. The rain descends in torrents, but we are perfectly dry. Our light tent does not leak a drop.

In half an hour the brief but fierce storm is over, the noonday sun out again in all his glory. We step outside. A light shower still falls in the woods from the surcharged leaves, while huge drops of water depending from the ends of limbs and sprigs of green moss are transformed into myriad gems by the bright sunshine. The merry whistle of the grey Canada bird and the *chickadee-dee* of the little titmouse as he hops from limb to limb are heard on every side, accompanied by the chirr of the red squirrel seated saucily on a limb overhead with tail laid along his back.

A short half hour, and the well-stretched tent is again dry and formed into a pack, the canoes are reloaded, and we are off. Only a very small portion of Ox-Tongue Lake is visible from the landing. As we paddle out from the shore we catch sight of the tossing waters of the rapid round which we portaged. Now a larger part of the lake opens upon the sight. Right in front is a hill densely covered with hardwood and hemlock, while a long narrow bay extends fully a mile to the south, terminating in a small, shallow, reed-covered marsh. We turn to the left in a northerly direction and steer for the head of the lake. Numerous small bays indent the shores, and the overhanging trees are beautifully mirrored in the water. Many huge trunks, with roots on shore and tops deeply sunk beneath the surface, are seen on every hand.

A short distance from the landing we pass a sandy shore on our right, a favourite campground of the deer hunters; but a recent fire, occasioned by a carelessly left campfire, has robbed it of the greater portion of its pristine beauty. Right opposite, on our left, a hardy settler has cleared a few acres, put up his little house, and endeavours to hew out for himself and family a home. The house is surrounded by Indian corn, potatoes, and vegetables. The oats growing in a small field, together with beaver hay, will furnish the winter supply of food for his cow.

Gradually, as we get out into the open lake, we begin to feel the effects of the stiff nor'wester, which, to use a nautical phrase, strikes right on the port beam. Our little vessel bobs up and down in the short rough sea, and we must keep her bow quartering to the waves to avoid being swamped in the trough between them. Hitherto we have been seated on the thwarts; now we crouch low down in the bottom to lower the centre of gravity. Both eye and arm must now faithfully do their duty. A moment's carelessness or the missing of a single stroke at the proper moment may lead to irretrievable disaster. We must not paddle too hard, or we will drive her under, but keep steadily at it, and as the huge swell comes rolling forward, lift her gently to it. The bow rises up, ships a few drops of water; the wave rolls under, lifting the stern, and she glides softly down on the other side and is ready for the next.

Thus we glide on up the lake, gradually approaching the west shore. We dare not look round; to do so might be fatal, for our canoe is a ticklish lady and demands all our attention. A buck quietly looks on from beneath the spreading boughs of a projecting cedar; but he is perfectly safe, and seems to realize the fact that we have other business on hand that requires all our attention. We must forgo the luxury of tempting venison steak till a more convenient season. The land in front is low and level, with a wide stretch of cedar swamp extending right down to the water's edge. A few tall balsams and still taller spruce, pine, and tamarack tower high above their fellows. A mile or so in the rear is a range of high hardwood hills extending away northerly in a line parallel to the shore. We are now well in with the land and out of the heaviest sea, and are able to shape our course in a more direct line up the lake. Right in front, another long narrow bay extends for a mile and a quarter beyond the head of the lake proper. Into its head empties a large brook, the outlet of Fatty's [Oxbow] and Dotty's lakes, each half as large as Ox-Tongue, the former in the township of Finlayson and the latter on the boundary between that and the township of Sinclair. On the west side of this bay is a strip of rich alluvial hardwood land. On the east the shore is composed of high hardwood and pine-clad hills.

We round a point, and the clearing of another pioneer is before us. The last settlers on the river, they are eight miles distant from the nearest neighbour. With a last look back at the little dwelling standing on that wild shore, we bid adieu to civilization. Getting abreast of the clearing, we are opposite the mouth of the river, to which we can now run across before the wind. We turn round to the right and for the first time catch a sight of the east shore. It is a series of high hardwood hills extending right down to the water's edge. In a little sand-fringed bay is a small abandoned clearing of an acre or two in extent. On our right is a low birch-clad island, another favourite camping ground for the deer hunter. No part of the backwoods is more famous for the number or fatness of its deer than the maple-clad hills that surround Ox-Tongue, and the blood of many a noble buck and graceful doe has dyed those waters in response to the rifle crack, as the fugitives bravely stemmed the waves in their flight from pursuing hound.

We pass to the right of a spruce-clad island with its surrounding bed of water lilies, and steer along the north shore, covered with stately red pine and dense undergrowth of balsam and hazel. We glide swiftly and smoothly over the seething waters. No danger now, as we run straight before the wind and have only to keep the canoe steady and straight on her course. In a few minutes we are at the mouth of the river. An ugly swell rolls as the current meets the wind-tossed waters of the lake. With a few more strokes of the paddles we pass into the smooth water beyond. We run into the west shore, where the bowman takes hold of a small project-ing alder and draws it underneath him. We rise gently from our recumbent positions and seat ourselves on the thwarts to ease our cramped limbs. The little vessel is now perfectly still, held in her place by the limb our bowman sits upon. Pipes are filled, and we take a smoke.

After a fifteen-minute rest, the alder limb is let go and we are again under way up the river, paddling easily against the gently flowing current. In a few minutes we pass to the left of a small dot of an island. At a distance it looks like a large alder bush, so com-pletely is the land concealed and the shore overhung by dense foliage. The banks of the stream are of only moderate height, and covered with large pines, birch, and balsam; the dry land here comes right to the water's edge, then again retreats a short way, leaving a few rods of marsh, covered with alder and tall beaver grass, elevated only a few inches above the surface of the stream and completely submerged at every freshet. Now we glide along a stretch of clear water; anon through a mass of long water grass, the tops swaying with the current, then over another stretch of deep water; again, all at once, it shallows up to only a foot or two in depth.

Hist! There is something moving yonder close into the shore beneath the projecting boughs of the alder bush. We glance in the direction indicated, and there a little brown head with sharp eyes moves swiftly upstream at a distance of only a few feet from the shore. A foot or so behind the head is a curved black object about the thickness of one's finger. Both ends are in the water, with the centre elevated a couple of inches above the surface in the form of a small arch. This is the tail of the little muskrat, the body being completely submerged. Suddenly both head and tail disappear, and he is off to his house underneath some projecting bank.

A little farther on we pass an alder floating down. It has been newly cut, for the leaves are quite green. We pause, and taking hold of it, lift it out of the water. It looks as if it had been cut with a pocketknife of some schoolboy. Each stroke of the knife—half a dozen or so—is distinct from the other. But a closer examination shows that the knife-marks, instead of being straight and smooth from the keen edge of the blade, are slightly rough and a little concave. It is the handwork, or rather tooth-work, of the beaver. The alder has been cut probably with intention of making it part of next winter's supply of provisions, but by some oversight it has been allowed to float down the stream—for beavers, like men, are occasionally careless—and it is consequently lost.

Again we encounter some wands, or pieces of alder and birch, the bark completely stripped off, every tooth-mark of the animal distinctly visible on the surface. On these master or mistress beaver has supped the previous evening. The animal lives exclusively on the bark of trees. The poplar is seemingly his favourite food, after which comes the alder and white birch.

Now we pass a large pile of alder and white birch saplings beneath the water, and close into the shore, where the soft alluvial bank has attained an elevation of a few feet above the surface of the water. This pile of brush is the beaver's supply of food for next winter. He has burrowed a hole in the adjacent bank for his castle, the entrance to which is down deep beneath the water, thence sloping upwards till it reaches the chamber in the interior of the dwelling, where it is both dry and warm. Here, if he is a newcomer, it has been the summer's work of himself and partner to prepare the home and gather the supply of provisions for the long and severe winter. Beavers never venture out while the river is frozen over, except to the brush pile, when after hauling a stick out of the water and eating off the bark, the trunk is thrust out and allowed to float away. Here the wily trapper knows exactly where to set his trap, which he fastens to a picket driven into the bottom of the stream. It must be put down in such a position that the animal, when caught, will be unable to drag the trap on shore, or he will in a very few hours release himself by cutting off his foot. Should he be successful in thus freeing himself, the wound quickly heals, and it is no uncommon thing for a beaver to be caught with both front feet gone, the fellow, like an old warrior, hobbling round on his stumps. It is here also during the winter months that they bring forth their young.

A little over a mile above the lake, having followed numerous sharp bends and windings, a roar of falling waters begins to be heard, gradually growing louder. The river narrows somewhat. We round a bend, where right in front is an inclined mass of dark shingle with water boiling and bubbling through the stones. We now turn abruptly to the right and shoot swiftly across in front of the fall in a rapid froth-covered current. To the left, the water rushes down amongst the boulders and round the roots of some large hemlocks and elms. Half a dozen strokes, and we wheel suddenly to the left. The next moment our bow runs up against the stones, and we are at a standstill. We have reached the end of the portage at the foot of the Ragged Falls.

In a few minutes everything is on shore, the packs shouldered, and we are off over the portage of ten or twelve chains. It is rather steep and rough, and owing to the ruggedness of the shore we are compelled to ascend a considerable distance higher than what is actually necessary to overcome the difference in water levels, and again descend to the shore at the head of the chute.

Round a little bend in the river is an old campground. Here, though it is still early, we will camp for the night, this being our first day out.

CHAPTER 6 NOTES    *In quick succession as it tumbles off the western lip of the Algonquin highlands, the Oxtongue River leaps over two magnificent falls—High Falls and, a short ways downstream, Ragged Falls. Both are today encompassed by Oxtongue River–Ragged Falls Provincial Park, established in 1985—exactly a century after the trip described in this book. Mighty, brawling Ragged, 25 metres high, ranks among the most spectacular of the cataracts on the rivers spilling from the Algonquin highlands. It is easily reached via a short access lane and trail off Highway 60 just east of Oxtongue Lake.*

*Apparently impressed to a greater degree by Ragged's trout-fishing potential than by its beauty, Dickson devotes more description to High Falls. This splendid chute boasts a dramatic setting deep in the forest, and even today the only easy public access is by canoe. Modern maps incorrectly label it Gravel Falls; it is, however, neither high nor gravelly (it is higher up the river, which may explain the name). It drops 9 metres, or 30 feet. Dickson stretches that to 40 feet in the book, but recorded 20 feet in his survey report. In 1893 the Gilmour lumber company constructed huge wooden troughs, called slides, to carry logs past the treacherous jam-prone chasms at both High and Ragged. Most traces of this intervention having vanished, the falls now look much as Dickson saw them.*

*Above High Falls, the Oxtongue lies on the plateau level of the Algonquin highlands. Consequently, the additional rise to the first headwater lake, 26 kilometres upstream, is modest. In this upper course the river meanders between high hills along the broad floor of a gently sloping valley, broken only by minor chutes, brief rapids, and shallow swifts. Along here Dickson refers to a South Branch entering, "nearly half as large" as the Oxtongue. This is Gateway Creek, actually only a seventh as big, but appearing larger at its mouth because it enters through an abandoned meander loop (oxbow) of the Oxtongue.*

*As nightfall approaches at the end of this chapter, the party crosses what is now the boundary of Algonquin Park, and makes camp little more than 2 kilometres southwest of the present site of the West Gate.*

# 6

## *Nature, Animate and Inanimate*

—◼ ◼—

IN HALF AN HOUR EVERYTHING IS OVER THE PORTAGE. WHILE CAMP IS
being pitched, we determine to look at the falls and see also if we
cannot add to our larder a few of the trout that we think ought to
lurk amongst the eddies of the chute—although the water is now
warm, and they will mostly have retired to the colder strata near
the bottom of the lake. A small hook is quickly made fast to the
end of a fine line ten or twelve feet in length, and, knife in hand,
we go into the woods and cut a maple sapling the same length as
the line. Securing also a piece of fat pork, we make our way back
to the foot of the falls. Climbing up over the big boulders to
where it takes its final leap, we find a deep dark pool at the foot of
a ledge of rock, beneath some huge trunks of pine borne down by
the spring freshets. On either side rise high granite rocks, below
which the falls spreads out somewhat and finally reaches the foot,
or smooth water, by narrow channels amongst the loose stones.
During the spring freshets or heavy rains of the fall it is a great
roaring flood, but now, at low water, we ascend easily without
wetting a foot.

The water boils and churns in the pool, such that one would
scarcely think even a trout could maintain its position in the
seething mass. Our line is quickly got ready, a small piece of pork
stuck on the hook, and it is cast in. Scarcely has it sank beneath

the surface when there is a sudden jerk and quivering. We give it a quick pull, and a speckled beauty dangles in the air. Our pocket-knife is again quickly out, a small crotched sapling cut, the fish taken off the hook, and one end of the crotch passed in through the gills and out at the mouth. Our first fish thus secured and laid safely to one side, the bait is replenished and again cast in. There are a number of the pot-like holes similar to this; we try them all in succession.

Smile not, professional angler, who believes that trout can only be taken with the fly. We have seen many a fine string of little beauties caught in this manner. The fish seem to have dashed at the swiftly moving bait and got caught before they felt the taste of this, to them, novel food. If by any means one of them has tasted it without getting hooked, you may bid him goodbye till you have something more tempting to offer.

Climbing over logs and stones, and casting the line into every pool or lump of froth as we pass, we make our way to the top of the falls, and finally regain the camp with a fine string of as lovely trout as one could desire. A half dozen willing hands are quickly at work. The fish are cleaned and placed in the frying pan along with the pork. In a few minutes supper is ready, and the scenes of the previous evening are enacted over again, while the merry jest and verse of song are heard on every side.

In due time all hands are in bed. The fire begins to burn low, the conversation all but hushes. The mellow light of the moon plays hide-and-seek amongst the tree tops gently waving to and fro in the night breeze. A night owl utters his hoot in a tree top hard by the camp, and a belated answer comes from a member of the same family on the other side of the river. Suddenly we hear a crackling of dry sticks a short distance behind the camp.

"Hist, boys; what is that?"

The welkin is now awakened by a shrill noise something between the toot of a horn and a whistle—a sound easily imitated by the mouth, but one which we, at least, cannot describe with the pen. It is the whistle of a deer. Immediately one of our most ardent hunters—one only in theory, making his first trip into the wilds—is up and undoing the rifle from the tent pole.

"Where are you going?"

"I'm going to shoot that deer."

"Well, you'd better take a grain of salt with you to put on his tail. He ain't agoin' to stand there looking at you and the camp till you get near enough."

Our amateur hunter is inclined to take this as something approaching an insult, and steps lightly out in bare feet, carefully, as he thinks, avoiding all dry limbs, and while avoiding one, as surely steps on two others, and larger ones. At last he stops, thinking he must be nigh the game, when after listening for full five minutes, another faint whistle is heard away in the distance. The deer has quietly walked off, no one knows how or when.

Our hunter now returns to the tent, grumbling in somewhat forcible language at having got his toes hurt by the brush. A half hour is now passed in listening to thrilling tales of deer hunting, or some wonderful exploits in tall shooting, when the conversation again gradually lags, and finally perfect silence reigns—a silence and calmness that we have never experienced anywhere except in the deep woods, broken only by the occasional whistle of the Canada bird or cry of the whippoorwill, the chirp of the tree frog, and roar of the adjacent falls.

It is another glorious morning, when in response to the "Hurrah, boys; breakfast!" we emerge towel in hand from the tent. The air in the early morning in the dense woods seems as if it were possessed of a peculiarly invigorating freshness which we have never felt in any other place. In half an hour breakfast is over. It is no daintily prepared meal of hot rolls, buttered toast, luscious beefsteak, and fresh eggs, washed down with well-creamed and sugared tea or coffee, but dry biscuit, baked beans, and fried pork, with a top dressing of cold apple sauce, and a dish of tea. It is a meal we could not eat at home, but just what we want here. And such a meal as we do make of it! Each man disposes of as much as would suffice for half a moderately sized family in town or city!

We have been considerably annoyed during the early morning by mosquitoes and black flies, and the insidious and almost imperceptible sandfly—but this is an annoyance we all knew we had to put up with, and has scarcely been as bad as was represented.

Immediately after breakfast, packing up is begun. A stranger would think, from the apparent confusion in which everything is lying around, that half a day at least would be consumed in the process; but each man knows his own blanket and his own share of the heterogeneous mass, and in another half hour the work is completed, and a number of neatly tied packs are all that are to be seen. Not a single article has been overlooked or forgotten. The embers of the fire are carefully scraped together, and, before the cookery is packed up, deluged with water. The dry turf that surrounded the fire is carefully examined and thoroughly wetted to drown out any scattered embers that, if overlooked, might remain smouldering for days and then break out into flame, destroying many miles of valuable timber and materially damaging the land as well. This care is imposed upon us by an Act of the Provincial Legislature to prevent the spreading of bush fires in certain localities. Were we to neglect it we would be liable to a heavy penalty.

A very few minutes suffice to load the canoes. Each is furnished with an axe, as we will likely encounter newly fallen trees or floodwood through which we shall have to cut our way. In a few minutes we are off, giving short, vigorous strokes with the paddle. A short, quick stroke is preferable in a bark canoe to a long steady pull, such as is best in a punt or skiff, because our little vessel is so light that as soon as the paddle is lifted out of the water her headway slackens.

Here the current is much more swift than it was below the falls, especially round the bends and where the higher banks come right down to the water. But the practised eye of the steersman sees on which side of the stream is the slowest current, or the little returning eddy, which is quickly taken advantage of. In about twenty minutes we see ahead a perceptible fall, or rather miniature chute, of a dozen yards or so in length. The water rushes through the half-submerged shingle, a bar of which extends out from either side, leaving a narrow canal of smooth swift water in the middle of the stream. Towards this narrow passage the water above converges fan-like, then rushes down in a smooth unbroken sheet, till at the foot it meets the retiring eddy on each side, whence it dashes away down the centre of the stream in a narrow, rippling, heaped-up ridge. Meeting the calm deep waters below, it spreads out, is absorbed, and vanishes. We gently propel our vessel up alongside this ridge close to the foot of the barrier of stones, when quickly and deftly we shoot the canoe into the middle. With a few skilfully directed and vigorous strokes we dash right up the centre, and the next moment are skimming swiftly and gracefully over the deep still waters above.

A little farther on, we glide over a smooth pond-like expanse bounded on either side by a narrow strip of low alder-covered land, bordered at the water's edge with luxuriant reeds and coarse grass. Another half mile, and the water ahead rushes swiftly but smoothly, broken only by tiny whirlpools, round a bend to the right. At the foot of this rapid a narrow opening in the woods at either side of the stream extends both easterly and westerly in a straight line. A blackened spot is seen on the trees that stand close to the open space, where pieces of the bark and timber have been hewn off. These marks, called blazes, have been made to show the line; this is the boundary between the townships of McClintock and Finlayson.

Impelled by the quick, skilfully plied strokes of the paddles, we quickly glide up the swift water round the little bend. Here we must be doubly careful, for though we must ply both swift and powerful strokes, there are many large stones scattered all round, with only an inch or two of water above them. To strike against the sharp edge of one at this speed would be fatal to our light vessel. After another half mile we have overcome one or two more of those little raceways, and are in another pond-like stretch with its margin of alder-covered marsh to the left. We perceive ahead in the distance the stream flowing swiftly round a bend to the left, and tumbling over and through a bed of large shingle elevated a couple of feet or so above the level on which we float. We keep along up the shore on our right, straight for a little sharp bend in the bank, with an eddy just about large enough to hold a couple of canoes right at the foot of the tumbling waters. Here we see some of our party engaged in unloading their canoes under a spreading birch.

The packs are again quickly transferred from canoes to shoulders. A three-minute walk across a narrow neck of land, and we find ourselves again on the side of the river. To follow it round the bend would be a full quarter of a mile, up which it would be impossible to propel the canoes. Here we meet the swiftly flowing river at right angles. During the spring floods it is a rushing, roaring stream ten or twelve rods wide, and at least twelve feet deep; now it is confined to a narrow channel of some sixty feet along the north bank. The remainder of the channel is now dry shingle, amongst which are many tufts of lovely tall ferns. Above this the stream comes in a broad shallow body round a bend from the east, and is spread out over the whole channel. The end of the portage on the other shore lies directly opposite, and as the water is too deep to wade, the canoes are again launched and ferried across. This is the foot of the High Falls portage. Once more we trudge off beneath our loads.

For a short distance the narrow path runs level, cutting off a bend of the river, glimpses of which we catch through the trees to the right. Now we are on the shore and ascending the side of a hill. A dull roar ahead has been gradually increasing, till at last, on reaching the top of the ridge, the noise becomes deafening. We lay down the packs to draw our breath and enjoy the view. Stepping to the brow of the bank, we catch our first sight of the High Falls. Away a few chains to the east, and at about the same level on which we stand—for we are now many feet above the river—a dark body of water rushes apparently right past the sharp angle of a perpendicular granite cliff. It dashes down a narrow iron-bound channel in two or three quickly succeeding leaps, full forty feet into an almost round basin bordered by shelving rocks. Gliding round to the other shore, it then rushes along the base of a perpendicular cliff fringed on top with cedar, hemlock, and pine.

Pieces of white froth at short intervals become detached from the mass at the foot of the fall, and twirl and bob away down the stream. They are now momentarily arrested by a projecting ledge of rock, or caught by an overhanging limb of a tree; then, shooting swiftly down a smooth stretch, are finally lost in the distance, where, deprived of the churning powers beneath, the upper bubbles collapse. After playing round for a short time in some little eddy, they become gradually absorbed in the surrounding water.

Returning, we resume our loads. Advancing by a crooked path up another elevation, then across a gully that extends by a narrow gap between the rocks down to the foot of the falls, we emerge on an old campground, a rod or two in extent, by the side of the river above the falls. The whole portage has a length of perhaps thirty chains. After a drink of ice-cold water out of a little spring we discovered in the rocky gulch we just crossed, and ten minutes indulgence in the amber-tipped briarroot, we are again off to the lower end of the portage for another load; in an hour or so everything is up to this point. The stream for the next sixty rods is so shallow and full of stones that we find it more convenient to carry our goods up along the north bank for that distance; and so, resuming the packs, we pick our way along a path we brushed out on a former trip, and deposit the burthen by the side of the still waters on a grassy plot beneath a drooping balsam. In a little while everything is got there except one light load.

By this time our cook has awaiting us the tin pail of hot tea, flanked by a pile of biscuit and plate of boiled pork, cut into large slices, laid out on an empty bag for a tablecloth. As usual, we are ready for dinner. Seldom, indeed, are the words "I am not at all hungry" heard when we are once fairly at work. Talk of your horn of brandy or glass of gin to whet the appetite! We have been vigorously plying the paddle, trudging over the rough portage, bending beneath a heavy load, breathing the pure air of heaven, and when thirsty drinking the pure water of the river. Our brows, nay, our whole bodies, have been "wet with honest sweat" ever since early morn. What need have we of any drink, of that soul- and body-destroying element that man's ingenuity has manufactured out of the fruits of the earth that God gave for wholesome bread, to give us a relish for our food? The vigorous attack on the plain but strong diet shows whether we are hungry or not, and the pail is quickly drained of its last drop.

After dinner we take a look at the falls from the top, which is only a few steps off. Here, immediately above the falls, the river is between two and three chains wide, when suddenly the shores turn almost at right angles to the stream. The water approaches in a smooth, deep, dark, unruffled mass to the very brink, where it is only a little over thirty feet wide; then it suddenly dashes from ledge to ledge away into the swirling eddy beneath—a mimic Niagara! What a spot for trout in the early spring, or late in the fall, when the fish come up out of the deeper waters of the lake.

We take an hour's rest, and perhaps a five-minute siesta—for the drowsy god is very apt to steal upon one as he reclines, pipe in mouth, beneath the shade of a friendly balsam. We had no intention of going to sleep. We did not think we were asleep till suddenly we start up from a state of obliviousness to find the pipe has slipped from our mouth. There it lies amongst the leaves where it dropped as the soothing deceiver stole upon us.

By this time the cook has everything that had been loosed again packed up. The loads are tossed upon the shoulders, and off we go. A few minutes suffice to reload the canoes, and once more we are under way.

Another short paddle over comparatively still water, a few swift strong strokes up another short rapid, a sudden bend to the right, and we reach another short rough spot; but by keeping close to the right bank we are able to thread our way amongst the stones by paddling and pushing alternately. A five-minute paddle brings us to another difficult place. This time there is only a very short portage on the south side—three or four chains long—and everything is quickly across. One of the canoes has been butted against a stone in the last rapid, and a small leak is the result. A few shreds of bark are torn from a neighbouring birch and laid out on the dry shingle in the bed of the river; some dry limbs are broken and laid on top, and a lighted match is applied. While one holds the ever-ready gum dish over the flame, others turn up the canoe, when a careful survey reveals the small leak. The surrounding bark is carefully wiped dry, then a burning brand is held over it. By the time the gum is melted, the bark is thoroughly dry. This is absolutely necessary, for the gum will not adhere to the bark if the latter is at all wet. In a couple of minutes the craft is once more watertight. The packs are again laid carefully in their places. Extra care is taken this time to make the seats comfortable, for it is a long pull to the next portage, and if we encounter much flood-wood and have long delays in consequence, it may be camping time before we can reach it.

We now glide smoothly and noiselessly along a deep dark stream upwards of two chains in average width, frequently pulling through heavy banks of long water grass. In many places the current is scarcely perceptible. The river is very crooked: now the sun is directly on our back, then on the left, again on the right; anon another sharp bend brings it almost directly into our faces, and the prow is aimed at every point of the compass in rapid succession. Here we are able to steer straight from point to point on alternate sides of the stream; there we must run half across the river to avoid the bushy top of a fallen balsam or spruce at some narrow bend. Everywhere the shore is lined right down to the water with overhanging alders and balsams, their lower limbs submerged. In the background are tall pines and spruce. There, on the north shore a short distance back from the river, rears a high hill clothed with a dense covering of heavy hardwood. It is soon left behind, but after another half-hour pull it is again almost directly in front, seemingly as near as before. Another sharp turn to the east, and we bid it a final goodbye.

"Hist! There's a duck just at yonder point."

We paddle gently up. Our bowman with gun in hand is ready for a shot. There she is—a shell duck with a dozen young ones no bigger than your fist. They now discover our approach. There is a sudden dash, and away they go, the old lady leading, followed closely by the little grey mites. Swiftly they dash along, faster than we can follow. Scarcely anything is visible save half a dozen streaks of sparkling white water. They are soon out of sight, and are seen no more, having diverged into some one of the numerous small lagoons that open out at short intervals all along the shore where the surrounding country is swampy.

There, right ahead, is the naked trunk of a great lofty pine, its roots resting against one shore, the top sticking against the other. It has been uprooted and brought down during the high water, and by some means swung athwart the stream, there to remain, either to be released by the next freshet or to form the key log of a mass of floodwood, gradually increasing in size as tree after tree is brought down and added to the pile. We cannot get round either end, but the centre of the tree is submerged. We may be able to run over it. Paddling slowly up, we find only two or three inches of water above the trunk at the deepest part, not nearly enough to float the canoe, deeply laden as she is. She is laid alongside. We step lightly out on the submerged tree, then bringing the bow up with one of us on either side, she is easily lifted over. We again step in, lay hold of the paddles, and resume our course.

Before going much farther we meet another obstruction. This time a dozen or more trees have got locked together, completely blocking the channel. Thickly growing alders overhang the mass of timber on both sides. Before we can begin to make a passage some of them must be cut out of the way. One of us is quickly on the shore, and the little craft made fast to a projecting limb. The obstructing bushes are soon cut and tossed into the water. After ten minutes work with axe and long pole, cutting, parting, and pulling, a narrow passage is cleared between the mass of floating timber and the shore, and pushing the canoes up the opening, we once more embark and are off.

We now skirt along by the side of a stretch of burnt land on our left. A dense mass of poplar and white birch, intertwined with red raspberry and thimbleberry bushes, completely covers the ground. Amongst these bushes are numerous tall blackened trunks of half-burnt pine and birch, varied by an occasional green top that escaped the devouring element. The fire took place some ten or twelve years ago, and was caused by the carelessness of some deer hunter or trapper.

Another mile along the winding stream we pass the mouth of a river coming in from the south side, nearly half as large as the one we are ascending. This is called the South Branch, and has its source some ten or fifteen miles to the southeast in the township of Livingstone. After passing this point we are for some distance clear of the marshy ground, and for the rest of this day's travel, at least, the current is much more strong, and our progress correspondingly slower. Besides, there are more frequent interruptions with tree tops and masses of floating timber. The sun is now getting low in the west; it is nearly six o'clock, and all hands are on the lookout for a proper spot to pitch camp for the night.

The river banks are here formed of either sandy loam or stiff clay with points of rock sticking out at short intervals, and have a perpendicular height of from six to ten feet. At length, reaching a spot where the land rises less abruptly from the water, we turn into the shore. An old and experienced hand leaps out and up the bank. For perhaps a couple of minutes he is out of sight. He then returns to the top of the bank with the welcome announcement, "This place will do very well, boys."

CHAPTER 7 NOTES    *Heavy rain causes the Dickson party to lay up for a day and spend two nights at the campsite on the Oxtongue River just inside the present boundary of Algonquin Park. Flies, of course, have always tormented campers; the "smudge" described in this chapter was a widely used, if somewhat drastic, remedy.*

*Never one to overlook a detail, Dickson tells of hanging their guns muzzle-down in the tent so that in the event of leaks, a drop of water won't fall into the barrel—sage advice, no doubt, in the day when a gun was standard equipment in the wilderness, and often relied upon to augment the otherwise monotonous regimen of pork and beans.*

*A considerable stretch of the Oxtongue River (on which the "rainy day camp" represents about the midpoint) flows through the southern and southeastern parts of Finlayson Township, first of the Algonquin highland townships surveyed by Dickson (in 1878). The rest of this township does not figure in the locale of* Camping in the Muskoka Region. *Unlike those farther east, Finlayson contains only scattered small lakes and, aside from the Oxtongue, no navigable streams—it is not an area of easy canoeing. The township wasn't included in Algonquin Park in 1893, but the eastern half was added shortly afterwards.*

*Dickson got a late start on his survey of Finlayson (July 29, 1878) and didn't complete the job until February 1879; on subsequent township surveys he finished in the fall. He may have reached Finlayson overland rather than by canoe: it lies adjacent to parts of eastern Muskoka being settled in the late 1870s. He certainly didn't leave Finlayson in a canoe!*

*In 1879 Dickson surveyed Ballantyne Township at the northwest corner of the Algonquin highlands (Kawawaymog–North Tea Lake area), then from 1880 to 1885 did six townships east of Finlayson, in the headwaters of the Oxtongue, Petawawa, and Madawaska Rivers. Thus in 1880 he first canoed the entire upper Oxtongue and first saw some of the highland lakes described in* Camping in the Muskoka Region.

*"Large black woodpecker" (page 96): pileated woodpecker. "Little bird with bosom red" (page 98): perhaps a rose-breasted grosbeak, or a robin.*

# 7

## *A Wet Day in Camp*

IN FIVE MINUTES EVERYTHING IS ON SHORE. THE CANOES ARE TAKEN out and turned bottom-up, and every man is busily employed at his allotted work. In less than an hour the tents are pitched, the beds prepared, and everything is made snug for the night. Our heavy boots having been removed, we sit round on moss-covered logs, or recline on the fragrant boughs of balsam, awaiting supper.

So far our only bread has been biscuit or hardtack, and there is now a general desire for a change. The cook passes the word that if we will but have a little patience he will make pancakes for supper. This offer is hailed with delight. A pail of water is hung over the fire; the necessary quantity of flour is emptied into the big tin dish, a handful of salt and the requisite portion of hot water are added, and the mass is stirred with a spoon into a thin batter.

Meanwhile, half a bake-kettleful of pork has been frizzling and frying; now cooked, the meat is lifted out and placed in a plate, and the boiled grease put in another. A quantity of the flour batter is poured in, and the kettle again placed on the fire. In a few minutes the underside is done, when it is divided into quarters by the big butcher knife, carefully turned, and replaced on the fire. In a few more minutes it is thoroughly cooked. The pieces are taken out, a quantity of grease is poured in, the bottom is again covered with the batter, and the same process gone through with till the cooking of the whole mass is accomplished. The vigorous attack, complimentary remarks, and empty plates bear ample testimony to the quality of the food.

Supper over and dishes washed, it is proposed to have some cakes for breakfast. Another visit is made to the bag of flour, and the necessary quantity, together with salt and water, emptied into the dish. This time a small portion of baking soda is added, and the whole kneaded into a dough. Both bake kettle and frying pan are this time called into service, carefully wiped clean, then rubbed over with grease to prevent the cakes from sticking to the metal. A piece of dough is laid in, carefully kneaded and flattened out on the bottom with the hand, for here there is neither rolling pin nor bake board. It is surprising how few articles we find absolutely necessary for our work, and how many heretofore deemed indispensable are discarded and done without. A few coals are drawn out from underneath the fire, the bake kettle set on them, and the lid ornamented with a light covering of the same material. The frying pan is propped up in a slanting position before the fire, with a shovelful of coals thrown down behind it. Care must be observed that the cooking process is not done too hurriedly, or a sodden, half-cooked cake with almost impenetrable crust will be the result of our labour. But our cook is master of the position, and in a remarkably short space of time a dozen rich, light brown cakes—the scones of our early childhood, and bannocks of the North-West—are ranged round cooling against trees and logs.

During the last hour the sky has been gradually becoming overcast. The cry of the large black woodpecker has been heard at short intervals all day. Low gusts of wind sweep up from the south and moan amongst the tree tops. The flies during the last half hour have become much more troublesome, while the tree frogs keep up an almost continuous chirping. The smoke from the fire, rather than rising in graceful spiral columns and melting away above the trees, floats in heavy masses down the river. Everything betokens the unmistakable approach of rain. It will be no sudden summer thundershower of only an hour or two duration, but a steady, even downpour that may detain us where we are for the whole of tomorrow. Our small dishes are piled bottom-up with the larger on top. The canoes are all right, for they were laid bottom-up when we landed. Care is taken to see that each part of the tent is evenly stretched, while every article that water can at all injure is put in a dry place. Nothing must be allowed to touch the canvas, or the water will soak through it. Everything is soon housed. The sides of the front part of the tent, hitherto turned back and left open, are drawn together and laced, and we sink to rest. There is no noise of tumbling waters for a lullaby tonight, for the slowly flowing river rolls noiselessly past; but we are lulled to sleep by the moaning of the wind amongst the giant mountain pines—grandest of music, and old as the everlasting hills.

About midnight we are awakened by the pattering of heavy drops of rain overhead. The wind has risen to a gale, and now howls through the trees. In a short space of time it is a steady downpour, now falling almost perpendicularly, next in a slanting direction, borne by the varying blast.

"Lie over, Hank; I'm jammed against the tent, and my shoulder is wet through," exclaims one suddenly awakened sleeper.

"By Jove, I left my socks outside to dry by the fire; I guess I'd better bring them in," says another. As the speaker hastily rises and stumbles out into the darkness, he is followed by the request to bring in a forgotten pair of pants from one quarter, and a shirt or hat from another. In a very brief space of time he returns, with such of the articles as he has been able to lay his hands on in the pitchy darkness. And, while securing a pair of half-dried socks or pants, he has succeeded in getting his own shoulders and feet completely soaked. He stumbles in, stepping on some leg or foot, evoking from the unfortunate owner sundry expressions most emphatically uttered, but hardly fitted for ears polite, and which always look bad in print.

In two or three places heavy drops of water fall from the tent. A match is now struck and a sperm candle lighted—we always carry a supply, and have one convenient to the hand every night on retiring to be ready in case of an emergency. The leaks are occasioned by small twigs or leaves that have fallen on the canvas. They are knocked off, when the drops at once cease. A careful survey of the interior is now made, and sundry articles that have moved are readjusted. The guns, which had been tied muzzle-up, are reversed to ensure no water getting into the barrels. Pipes are lit all round and a midnight smoke is indulged in. A half hour of conversation and badinage ensues. The subject recalls reminiscences of similar nights spent on some lonely island or river shore. The candle is extinguished, and all is again hushed in slumber's soft calm.

With the first streak of dawn we are attacked by myriad mosquitoes and black flies. They are always worst either immediately before or during rain. In a few minutes all hands are awake and stirring. We step to the door, undo the fastenings, and look out. What a contrast between this morning and yesterday! Then, while the first rays of the rising sun turned the tree tops a bright golden yellow, we were greeted with the whistling of the "little bird with bosom red," the shrill cry of the blue jay and other kindred songsters, and the merry chirping of the squirrel as he gambolled from bough to bough or chased his mate round the gnarled trunk of a neighbouring birch. Now, all animated nature is hushed. A wild gale howls amongst the trees, threatening wreck and ruin to many a stately forest monarch. The rain descends in torrents. The surface of the river tosses and tumbles in a million little globules as the big descending drops strike the water. A heavy, dark, impenetrable veil hangs over all, with thin fleecy patches of clouds scudding before the raging gale. A thick whitish mist hangs low amongst the trees and over the river. Everything betokens a wet day.

The flies are almost beyond endurance. A man steps outside and after a short search succeeds in getting a handful of dry chips and bark. The door of the tent is again closed, a small space of ground cleared at the back end, and a fire started. As soon as the dry chips have kindled into a blaze, damp moss and leaves are laid on top. The flame is at once extinguished, giving way to a dense cloud of smoke. This is what woodmen call a smudge. No variety of the fly family can live with it—nor can man while it is so dense. So the door is again opened, and a thick volume rolls out, and with it also the flies. One or two with towels or hat in hand drive them from the corners. The smudge is now reduced to more moderate dimensions, so that it will give forth only a light smoke that we can breath without much inconvenience, and we resume our couch for another snooze.

Our sleep is not of long duration, however, for the cravings of hunger are felt, and we must eat. The cook, enveloped in a waterproof, soon has the tea kettle merrily boiling. We must all bestir ourselves, for it is the rule of the camp that none shall eat till he has performed his morning ablutions. The blankets are carefully rolled up to prevent their being trodden upon by dirty boots. A hasty toilet is performed, and we are ready for breakfast. The rich steaming mass of baked beans is set down on the brush in our midst, flanked by the pail of tea and pile of bannocks. Our ever-thoughtful cook had made provision the previous evening for the protection of the bake kettle from the anticipated rain by placing a log on each side of the "pot-hole," and laying on top of them a sheet of bark stripped from a neighbouring hemlock, to prevent the fire from being drowned out.

Breakfast is soon disposed of, and we now recline at our ease patiently awaiting the ceasing of the rain. But reclining in perfect idleness we can only endure for a very limited period. In a short while a pack of cards is produced by one, and a euchre party is quickly formed. A few who are fond of reading unearth from some mysterious corner a book or two, while others, needle in hand, are at work replacing a lost button, mending a torn shirt or a pair of dilapidated pants, or darning a sock. Another, who had not taken the precaution to have tacks put in the soles of his boots before leaving home, has made the discovery that the smooth soles are rather slippery when wading amongst the wet stones. This intelligence is communicated by the company in general, as he ruefully compares the covering of his pedal extremities with those of his more thoughtful companions.

"I have a box of Hungarian tacks," says one, "and will give you some."

The offer is gladly accepted, and he is speedily at work driving them in with the pole of our lightest axe. The work is not such as would be turned out of a first-class shoemaker's shop, but they are at least driven well home, and will answer the purpose very well, though the rows may be a little irregular.

About nine o'clock the rain slackens; the weather begins to clear, and there are some prospects of a fine day yet, as small rents are seen in the dark mass of overhanging clouds. All hands step outside for a look. The mist has risen to the tree tops and hangs in white wreaths; small detached portions are still higher, while the wind has become almost entirely hushed. Those on their first trip volunteer the opinion the rain is over, but the older hands know better, for long experience has taught them that when the mist ascends after rain, it is sure shortly to descend again in more rain.

So the cook is informed that we shall not move today, at least not before noon, and he will have time to make a pot of pea soup, and also to boil some rice for dinner. The predictions as to the weather are soon verified. The rent clouds close up. Again the wind howls through the woods, and down comes the rain heavier than ever. We gladly return to our snug quarters inside. There is another lull in the storm between eleven and twelve o'clock, and again about one, during which we partake of the plate of rich and wholesome soup, with a top dressing of rice pudding and bannocks, and the never-overlooked dish of tea.

The weather now settles down to a steady afternoon of rain. The wind has entirely gone down, and perfect silence reigns, save only the pattering of the rain on tent and leaves. The afternoon is spent in chaff and chatter, interspersed by an occasional song. The cards are kept steadily going, one party succeeding another in rapid succession, while the consumption of tobacco is something beyond all conception.

A wet day is the only one that seems long in camp; the hours drag wearily along. About four o'clock the steady pour of the last three hours gradually begins to slacken; by another hour, small spots of deep blue sky become visible. There is a general lightening in the west. A beautiful rainbow glows against an eastern hill. The merry whistle of birds and the chirping of squirrels are again heard. The whole western hemisphere is now clear, the sun setting in all his glory, while yonder dark mass of clouds moves slowly but steadily towards the east. The dark foliage of the woods seems to have put on a darker and richer green, and all Nature seems to rejoice at having had its thirst quenched by the refreshing rain. By sundown the last vestige of cloud has disappeared. Gradually, as the shades of evening gather round, countless twinkling stars begin to shine on the sleeping face of Nature, while myriad fireflies emit their flashes in all directions. We retire to rest in the full confidence of a bright tomorrow.

CHAPTER 8 NOTES    *A ranger today would not be amused if he or she caught canoe trippers in Algonquin behaving as members of Dickson's party do, shooting enthusiastically at moose, ducks, and ruffed grouse as they continue up the Oxtongue River. But in the 1880s the wilderness, still considered virtually limitless, was regarded by both pleasure seekers and working woodsmen as a handy source of food and materials. Indeed, many early travellers took great pride in their ability to "live off the land"—quite opposite the modern philosophy of taking nothing but pictures and memories. (Well, maybe a few trout and blueberries, too!)*

*At Lower Twin Falls (lowermost of some small falls on the Oxtongue near the West Gate), Dickson scares up what he calls a crane, but this was actually a great blue heron. The partridge shot later on was a ruffed grouse. The red deer referred to in this and other chapters are the familiar white-tailed deer. Moose, though big, are not quite the largest mammals on the continent, as Dickson states—bison take that honour. However, they were then, and still are, the largest in Algonquin.*

*Blockages of floodwood, often necessitating portages, were common on the upper Oxtongue until 1893 when the Gilmour lumber company cleared the river out to allow for driving logs down it. A meandering stream like the Oxtongue, in many places actively eroding sandy banks on the outside of its curves, will naturally get an unusually large number of trees falling into it. Relatively shallow water and the numerous bends created ideal conditions for this material to jam up.*

*At the end of the day's paddle described in this chapter, the Dickson party camps at Whiskey "Falls" (more accurately called Whiskey Rapids now). Attributed to log drivers by Audrey Saunders in* Algonquin Story*—supposedly they upset a canoe in the rapids and lost a keg of whisky—the name more likely originated with trappers or hunters, or perhaps with Dickson himself: it was not until the spring of 1894 that the first log drive came down the upper Oxtongue. In* Names of Algonquin, *George Garland suggests the whisky-like colour of the water could have inspired the name.*

# 8

## *Hunting, Successful and Unsuccessful*

THE HEAVY MIST THAT HAS RISEN FROM THE WET SURFACE OF THE earth is being slowly dispelled by the rising sun as we emerge from our tent in the early morning. Every small tree and bush seems to have been invaded during the night by a host of spiders, and is almost completely covered by their webs, glinting in the sunshine. A gentle, invigorating breeze blows up the river, lifting and driving before it the heavy banks of mist from the surface of the water. Breakfast is speedily disposed of, and the packs are done up; but the tent is saturated with water and will require drying before being folded up. A big fire is made. The crutches that support the tent are driven into the ground a few feet from the fire, one set at each end, and the ridge pole is laid on top. Over this the tent is spread, in charge of two men to guard against it being burned. They turn it as soon as one side is dry, and in less than half an hour it is perfectly dry.

By seven o'clock everything is on board, and once more we stem the current of the river. The canoes bound lightly on their course, the water parting before them, giving forth a light swish as they dart ahead at each stroke of the paddle. The river becomes more crooked than it was below this point, and the current more swift, especially as it circles round the sharp bends. Now we pass a sandbank, covered on top with rank, coarse grass by the side of a small lagoon that extends a chain or two from the river. It is literally covered with deer tracks. But what are those as large as an ox's and sunk deep into the sand? There are no domestic cattle here. They are the footprints of the lordly moose, largest of all the wild animals of the continent, for we are now within his haunts.

After an hour of lively pulling, and rounding another sharp bend to the left, we see a few rods ahead the whole channel completely choked with the white trunks of trees, from the large pine to the small alder. We have a couple of times this morning already had some difficulty in getting past a single tree, but managed to make our way without having to get out. But this time the fact of there being a well-defined portage to the right is proof positive that we must unload. We step on the shore, where we get a better view of the mass of timber. The whole channel is filled for fully twenty rods with all sizes and varieties of trees, logs, etc., piled together in every conceivable shape, and in most places solid to the bottom, the water boiling and bubbling amongst them. Those masses of driftwood will frequently remain in one spot for years; then perhaps the whole will move down to the next bend, or portions of it will be loosened and move down to form separate jams at other points. What we found last year as one large mass we may now meet in three or four different places, with spaces of clear river between. Each creates a new and unexpected obstruction, rendering it impossible to make the estimated distance in a day.

Three-quarters of an hour is consumed in making this portage, reloading, and getting a fresh start. In another half hour a similar obstruction bars our way, when there must be another getting out and portaging across the point of land—for those masses of floodwood are almost invariably met with at bends in the stream. We reload, and once more the paddles ply swiftly and our little vessels bound gaily along the quickly flowing river. Now we avoid an overhanging limb, and then we must evade a sunken snag, one end of which rests on the bottom, the other on a level with the surface, its presence indicated only by a slight ripple in the water. It is the special duty of the man in the bow to guard against those hidden dangers, for nothing will more speedily or irretrievably ruin a canoe than to strike—while sailing fast—against the sharp point of one of those hidden snags.

After another ten minutes pull, we hear the roar of falling water, gradually increasing as we approach. A bend opens out into a small pond of an acre or two in extent. We keep along near the shore to our left, skirting a thin fringe of tall reeds. As in nearly all similar spots, a small creek winds its way into the river through a border of alders. We see a tall bluish-coloured bird with long legs, neck, and bill standing in the shallow water near the head of the bay. It is a crane engaged in the enjoyment of its morning meal on luckless frogs and small fish that may come within reach. We have hardly entered the bay when its quick eye detects our approach. One glance satisfies him that the moving objects are most to be admired when seen at a distance, and for his own safety he had better be going. There is a quick bending of the long, dark brown legs till the whole body nearly touches the water, then a sudden spring and unfolding of the long wings, and he rises almost perpendicularly into the air. The long limbs hang straight down till a sufficient altitude has been attained; the long neck assumes a similar position in front, and with slow and steady flaps of the huge wings, the stately bird sails slowly away up the valley of the river.

But his sudden flight has alarmed another feathered denizen of the water, hitherto concealed amongst the tall reeds. There is a quacking and whirr of wings, and a big black duck speeds quickly after the crane. Its young ones, whose wings are not sufficiently developed to support their fat bodies in air, scud to cover, warned by the cry of the fleeing parent that danger is nigh. A few of them would prove a welcome addition to our larder, for though unable to fly, they are more than half grown; but with all our woodcraft we might spend a whole day, and then fail to discover the retreat of a single one of them.

On the right, and away up at the head of the bay, we see the white water tossing and tumbling over great boulders, a few green alders and ferns forming a small island in the centre [Lower Twin Falls]. We are soon in the little eddy, and are borne gently up to the landing at the foot of the short portage. It is the old story over again. The stream dashes through a narrow gorge, formed by projecting rocks on either side, which contract it to less than one-fourth of its average breadth. For a distance of four or five chains it rushes and tumbles over a fall of eight or ten feet. In the next half mile we have two more of those short portages, besides one where, by moving a few stones, we can lead the canoes up the short chute without unloading. By the time we are over the last portage, sundry cravings and a feeling of emptiness in the region of the belt warn us that our inner man requires replenishing. As a long stretch of uninterrupted navigation is now before us, we conclude to take dinner before embarking. Wet socks are replaced by dry ones, and one or two small leaks attended to while the tea pail boils.

At the end of the usual hour for dinner we once more get off. Our best shot is given a ten-minute start, for this is not only the hottest season of the year, but also the time when the flies are at their worst, driving both deer and moose out of the thick woods to stand and wade in the shallows alongside the frequent fringe of tall beaver grass that lines the shores. The moose are fond of the large leaves of the water lily, which almost completely conceal the surface. The stream is now for some distance much wider, and has a slower current; and at a little distance the high dry banks give place to low muddy shores covered with alder and balsam.

Hearing the report of a gun ahead, and quickening our stroke as we round a bend, we perceive the canoe lying in by the shore with only one man in her. In answer to our query we are informed that, on rounding the last bend, they saw a large moose standing in the water and feeding on the water lilies. They had stolen up as near as they could without alarming him. When Jack fired, the huge brute stumbled to its knees, then sprang up and dashed off in amongst the alders. Jack is now off in pursuit of the noble game.

The canoes are quickly run in, and all hands leap on shore. There are the large ox-like tracks sunk deep in the soft mud, and we also are off along the trail. It is easily followed, even without looking down to the tracks, for the great brute has made a wide opening in his hurried retreat through the thick mass of alders. He is wounded, sure enough, for there are the fresh blood stains on the green leaves. We soon clear the alders and ascend the side of a pine-clad hill. It is easy following the trail by the big hoof prints and the sticks and leaves dashed aside in the hurried rush, and by the big drops of fresh blood. We have only gone a short distance farther when we meet Jack returning for instructions as to whether he shall continue the chase.

A hurried consultation is held. He informs us that he fired at the neck, expecting to either break it or cut the jugular vein. But the fact of its having risen at all after being shot is demonstrative evidence that the neck has not been broken, and by the way it is bleeding it is equally evident that the jugular vein has not been injured. It is consequently only a flesh wound, not at all likely to prove fatal; therefore to follow would be a wild-goose chase. The moose when thoroughly alarmed will trot continuously for many hours. Besides, a red deer would be preferred at present, for our small party could dispose of only a small portion of the six or seven hundredweight of dressed moose carcass before the rest of it spoiled at this season. We could easily make use of a whole red deer before any of it could become tainted. Jack is duly cautioned not to fire again unless he is sure he can lodge the bullet in a vital part, and is then given another ten-minute start.

After traversing another half mile, on rounding a bend, our hunters are again overhauled, resting on their paddles. They inform us that they have seen another moose, but as his position was not such as would ensure a fatal shot from the canoe, they had not fired, though less than half-gunshot distance from him.

"What did he look like, boys?"

"Oh, a great big brute of dark grey colour, as large as a horse, with a big clumsy head, thick heavy lips, and ears like a mule's."

Another half mile, another little spurt at a short rapid, and again smooth water, the shores still lined by the ever-present alder and balsam; now also we see occasionally a clump of willows and high cranberry bushes. A few miles of this, and the hard dry land begins again to gradually close in to the edge of the water, rising to low hills and knolls timbered with pine and white birch, with here and there a mountain ash, the rowan tree of Scotland.

Now we have before us a short straight stretch of river flowing swiftly between high sandy banks. All our strength has to be put forth to propel the little vessel against it. In a little while we reach the foot of a short rapid. Part of the load is landed and carried up a few rods to the smooth water above. Returning, we step into the water and lead the canoes up with the balance. The eastern boundary of the township of Finlayson crosses the river in the middle of this rapid; we are now in the township of Peck. Another five-minute paddle brings us to another floodwood portage. Like the others, it is soon overcome. Here the river well retains its width, but is visibly becoming shallower. Numerous waterlogged trees with dangerous projecting limbs encumber the bottom, and are half covered with sand.

For the next mile our progress is very slow, owing to the

numerous fallen trees. Here we have to shove through between the end of one and the shore, there lift over another, or cut a piece out of a third. A sudden quacking, and another duck darts off up the stream, while a dozen young ones, nearly as large as their parents, hurry to and fro trying to conceal themselves amongst the floating timber. A quick shot is taken, and a couple, after briefly spluttering and floundering, float dead on the water. All the others have suddenly and mysteriously vanished, we know not where, but a ten-minute search fails to discover a single head. The dead are picked up. They are found to be plump and fat, and will make an agreeable addition to the supper table.

In a little while our ears are again saluted with the noise of falling water as the river, hemmed in between overhanging cliffs, dashes over an obstructing ledge. We paddle in amongst the stones at the end of the portage on the north shore and land at the foot of Whiskey Falls. The sun is now sinking low in the west. Our watches are consulted; to our surprise, we find the hands indicate six o'clock. It is time to camp. Between paddling and pushing we have covered a good distance during the day; all are tired and also, as a matter of course, hungry. In a very few minutes everything is on shore, and each man at his allotted task in getting up the tent and putting everything in order for the night.

Along a perpendicular cliff on the opposite shore is a deep eddy dotted over with lumps of white froth. There ought to be trout there, close in to the foot of the fall. In a few minutes a hook and line are rigged. Launching a canoe, we paddle across to the foot of the eddy, then float up and step out on a half-submerged stone. By the time the work on the tents is finished, and the pork for supper is frying, a half dozen speckled beauties flop about in the bottom of the canoe, and we again embark and recross to camp. The ducklings have been plucked, cleaned, and quartered. Our fish are soon cleaned and deposited in the boiling grease after the pork has been taken out. Before putting in the trout they are rolled in flour; while cooking, a little salt and pepper are added. This may not be the orthodox method of cooking young ducks and fresh trout, but before you condemn it, gentle reader, just try one of the fish or a leg of duck; if you will then say you ever tasted anything more delicious, or made a heartier meal, we will admit the cooking a failure. By this time, as the bannocks have been all disposed of, we are again down to the never-failing and ever-ready hardtack. But, as the evening is fine, the cook has time to prepare a pot of rice for tomorrow's breakfast in addition to the apple sauce and pork.

There is no idling or dozing in bed in camp for two or three hours after sunrise. We retire with the first grey dusk of evening now that we are fairly in harness. And the first rays of the rising sun are just beginning to gild the upper limbs of the giant pines when all are again astir. During the night an awakened sleeper had heard a partridge drumming a short distance behind the tent. The bird is again heard while we engage in our toilet. A man picks up the double-barrel and steals quietly away towards the noise. He proceeds a few rods, then pauses to listen for a repetition of the sound, to find out on which of the numerous upturned trees the gay Lothario has chosen to sound his love notes. In a few minutes the drumming is repeated. Before the swiftly moving wings have ceased their motion, the quick eye of the woodman locates the spot. There he is on yonder old pine. The gun is at once brought to the shoulder, for one is generally within shooting distance before he gets sight of the game in those thick woods. The echoes of the report reverberate amongst the rocks. There goes a shower of feathers. The bird tumbles headlong to the ground; there is a brief fluttering of wings and kicking of feet, and the man triumphantly returns with the first partridge shot by the party.

CHAPTER 9 NOTES   *For four days Dickson has been ascending the Oxtongue, but from Whiskey Rapids it's only a short paddle to the first headwater lake, Tea, where the party lunches at the portage around Tea Falls at the outlet (now the site of the Tea Lake Dam picnic grounds) before proceeding up to a campsite on the west shore of Canoe Lake.*

*In 1893 the Gilmour lumber company built a dam at Tea Falls which raised Tea, Bonita, and Canoe lakes nearly 2½ metres, turning the shoal-filled river between them into a strait navigable by large boats. The turbulent creek from Smoke Lake was similarily flooded out. On Tea Lake Dickson mentions "a long narrow streak of red felspathic sand" on the north side—likely the beach at present-day Camp Tamakwa, much more exposed then due to lower water levels. The colour probably came from reddish-purple garnet.*

*The arrival of the lumbermen in 1893 abruptly destroyed the pristine wilderness character of the Tea–Canoe area, but even in the early 1880s increasing signs of human activity were evident—trapping, fishing, and especially surveying (Dickson subdivided this area, Peck Township, in 1880). But Dickson could hardly have foreseen that before the century ended, two mansions would stand on Gilmour Island in Canoe Lake, and a huge sawmill, village, and several kilometres of railway sidings would occupy the nearby northwest shore. Indeed, ever since the 1890s, Canoe Lake has been a hub of activity on the highlands.*

*A description of baking bread and frying fresh trout at the Canoe Lake camp will make many a mouth water. The fish were caught by night line, an effective—but now illegal!—technique described in some detail. Dickson's fish nomenclature may confuse some readers: he refers variously to speckled, brook, lake, and salmon trout. All, however, were of just the two trout species, lake trout and brook trout, native to waters on the Algonquin highlands. Both may be found in Algonquin lakes, but brook trout spawn in streams and also live in suitable ones. Trout belong to the same family as salmon. Today, contrary to Dickson's apparent usage, the name speckled trout is applied to brook trout.*

# 9

## *Canoe Lake and Naturalist Notes*

As usual, but a brief period suffices to dispose of breakfast and packing up. The packs and canoes are shouldered, and we are off across the short portage. Heavy drops of dew shower down upon us from hazel bush and alder as we brush along the narrow path. Here the landing is small, by the side of a shelving rock, and we can only load one canoe at a time; each, when ready, proceeds on its way.

But what pattering is that we have heard on the hillside all morning, as if some animal were taking a single heavy step at a time and then coming to a full stop? Gun in hand, we go up the bank to have a look and try to find out what it is. Pausing beneath a tall green pine, we listen. Suddenly the noise is repeated close behind us. Wheeling round to look, it is again repeated, a little to one side this time. Next we feel a sharp slap on one shoulder, when, looking up, one of the green cones that grow near the top of the pine just misses our face. We step a few paces to one side for a better view and look up. The mystery is at once explained. High up in the very top, where the cones are most numerous, a tiny squirrel runs from limb to limb nipping off cone after cone with his sharp teeth; if we chose to remain long enough, we would see the little gentleman run headfirst down the tree, seize one of the newly plucked cones, seat himself on a log, and holding the cone between his forepaws, tear off the green husks with his teeth and make his breakfast of the soft white pith within.

Having satisfied our curiosity and solved the problem of the peculiar noise, we retrace our steps to the landing, and in a few minutes are again under way. The stream is now a series of short stretches of smooth deep water alternating with shallow rapids, varying from a foot to three or four inches in depth. It is a continual repetition of getting out and in, paddling or pushing with the paddle along the deeper parts, and leading the canoe up the shallows. The bottom of the stream is composed of reddish-brown gravel. After a mile and a half of this, which consumes most of the forenoon, as we have frequently to take out part of the load, we enter a little bay. At the head of it a couple of pine trunks extend almost completely across the river, leaving a channel of only a few feet at the north shore. On reaching this point we have again to resort to wading for a few yards. During the last quarter hour we have heard the gradually increasing noise of a chute; on rounding the end of the pine trunks, and passing beneath an overhanging birch, the fall bursts upon our view as it rushes down a narrow rock-bound gorge. We climb into the canoe, paddle across a deep little bay to a flat rock almost even with the surface of the water, and step on shore at the end of a well-worn portage on the south side of the river. Above us, at a distance of three chains, lies the foot of Tea Lake.

This is the last portage we shall meet until a mile and a half above Canoe Lake. As we intend to go only as far as an old campground about halfway up that lake tonight, and there spend tomorrow, the Sabbath, we conclude to have dinner at the head of this portage. We take advantage of the pause to dry our garments.

Here the river rushes through a narrow gorge in the dark granite rocks, falling about nine feet in a distance of three chains. It is so rough and full of stones that no canoe or punt could run it, even when at the highest. At the proper season of the year this is one of the best spots on the whole river for trout fishing. Not only the small brook trout, but also the large speckled trout of the lakes may be taken in unlimited numbers.

The midday meal is quickly despatched, the usual smoke indulged in, dry clothing donned, then the canoes are reloaded. Only a short narrow neck of the lake is visible from the landing. The first few rods above the falls are so completely filled with stones that there is no small amount of difficulty in guiding the canoes safely through. In a few minutes, however, we are clear of obstructions and into deep water, and soon we enter a larger bay. Straight ahead, a small piece of second-growth timber marks the spot where at some former time a hunter's camp stood. Rounding a point of rock on the south shore, a small but lovely sheet of water lies before us. Right in our path, at the distance of three-fourths of a mile, a small pine-clad island rears its head high out of the water.

We can see all the south shore, which is comparatively straight, right to the head; and as we proceed, the north shore gradually opens to the view, extending away to the northeast in a series of points and small bays, where also there is a long narrow streak of red felspathic sand. The land nearly all round rises abruptly from the water's edge to moderately sized hills. A fringe of low, dark green cedar and balsam overhangs the water all round the shore, while a dense forest of hardwood and hemlock covers the hills, an occasional cluster of white pines rearing their heads high above all others. As we get fairly into the open lake, our light vessel begins to feel a fresh northerly breeze, and dances merrily over the tiny wavelets.

There to the right, a number of trees have been cut down; their brown tops lie in the water. As we pass by them we see a narrow open lane extending away up the hill to the south. Glancing to the north, a similar line is seen in that direction also. It is one of the many surveyor's lines that mark the limits of the farm lots into which the land has been divided. This whole section has been laid out into one-hundred-acre lots, and lines cut straight through the woods at right angles to each other at a distance of one hundred chains apart.

We glide past the south side of the island, and discover another smaller one immediately to the east of it. On our right, a spot of coarse grass and reeds marks the mouth of a modest creek, the outlet of a small lake [Coot] lying in a hollow amongst the woods half a mile to the south. On the smallest island are the traces of an old campground. A rude frame of poles raised a few feet above the surface of the ground denotes where fishing parties have dried the fish they caught at the outlet, to prepare them for being taken home—a treat for their city friends.

In a few minutes we emerge from the lee of the islands and must cross a neck of rough water; but it is soon passed. We now skirt the shore of a lovely hardwood point. Away half a mile to the east, a large brook rolls out from amongst the trees. It is the outlet of Smoke Lake, which lies a mile and a half beyond. Advancing round the point to the left, we soon reach the mouth of a narrow bay extending a quarter of a mile northwards. At its head a solitary pine, standing on a slight elevation in a lily-fringed marsh, points out the mouth of the river. A ridge of hardwood extends all along its west shore, while on its east side is a forest of tall pines.

The river is still a couple of chains wide, with a bright sandy bottom. The water is shallow and clear, and we pass over several shoals of trout lying near the bottom. A short half mile upstream we enter a pond [Bonita Lake] stretching like a huge bag for nearly half a mile to the east. We steer along the north side, round a grass-covered sandy point, and again enter the river, which extends away northeasterly along the base of a high rocky hill on the east side. A few rods from the mouth, a bar of stones almost completely fills up the channel; but steering close by the east side of a big boulder, we find a narrow passage sufficiently deep for our little vessels. Now a big creek, the outlet of some beaver pond away amongst the western hills, glides in through a bed of tall ferns. The river becomes much deeper, and has a black muddy bottom. The west shore is for the most part low and swampy, while on the east are high pine-topped bluffs.

There, a little dark brown animal runs along the shore. It is about the length of ordinary-sized cat, but with shorter legs, a somewhat smaller body, and a black bushy tail. It has not observed us before plunging into the water, bound, evidently, for the opposite shore, and we can see nothing but the round bullet head and a pair of sharp eyes. It is a mink, but we refrain from taking a shot, as the fur is almost worthless at this season. Suddenly the quick, piercing eyes catch sight of us, down goes the little head, and he is off in another direction.

Away at some distance ahead a reddish-brown animal, as large as a good-sized dog, walks out on a fallen tree that rests on the surface of the water. We stop and look at the animal through the field glass. It proves to be a large wolf. He has already caught sight of us as unfamiliar objects, but he is safe—too far off even for a rifle shot, especially when fired out of a canoe. After surveying us for a few minutes, he walks leisurely back to the shore and skulks away into the woods.

Our attention is now attracted to an object on shore, a few feet from the water's edge. A number of short pickets have been driven into the ground close to each other, leading out about a foot from the root of a tree. At a distance of six inches from this is another similar row parallel to it. The pickets are about one foot in height; on top are laid a few small balsam limbs. This is what is termed a mink house. A small steel trap is set at the door with a few leaves laid carelessly over it, so as to conceal it from the intended victim. A fish, piece of muskrat, or leg of partridge is fastened at the back end of the house. As the little animal reaches in for the bait, one of his legs is sure to be caught in the iron clasp.

Half a mile up, the stream shoals to about a foot in average depth, again with a bright sandy bottom. Pulling round to the left of a small island, and over the top of a bed of tall reeds, we see a large opening, when, on rounding a couple of bends, Canoe Lake is before us in all its picturesque beauty, extending away a little east of north. Right ahead, and at the distance of a mile, is a large rock-bound island [Gilmour], covered with graceful red pine. Only that portion of the west shore south of the island is visible from this point. Away to the east the land is high and mountainous, topped with a dense forest of pine. The brisk northern breeze has raised a heavy swell, and long white-capped waves chase each other into the mouth of the river. We are soon into it, our canoes dancing over the swells.

Our way is straight up the lake to the west of the island. The sea is very rough, but we think we can weather it. We edge as closely as possible to the west shore in order to be in shallow water in case of accident. But scarcely are we well out of the river, passing close by a low moss-covered rocky point on our right, when a loon suddenly plunges screaming into the water, and propelled both by foot and wing, dashes out into the open lake. She must have a nest near here. The loon, having no joint in the leg, cannot walk, and is never found on shore far from water. We run in behind a sheltering ledge of rock and step on shore. There on the bare ground, a few feet from the water, is a little black ball of down, scarcely bigger than a lady's clenched hand. A small black bill and pair of sharp eyes are visible on the upper side of it. The little fellow is evidently only a few hours out of the broken shell, which lies to one side. He has not yet taken his first bath, likely because he is waiting for his sibling, whose chirpings are heard issuing from another egg hard by.

Loons are very numerous in all these northern waters. They arrive as soon as the ice goes out in the spring, then return south again in October. As they cannot walk, they are never met with on land, but manage by the aid of their wings to flop a few feet on the shore and lay their one or two eggs on the bare ground. As soon as the young hatch they take to the water, and the tiny black dots may be seen following the old one round, or seated on her back. She feeds them with newly caught fish.

Our progress up the lake is exceedingly slow, for if we put on too much speed we will in all probability be swamped. A long narrow bay extends away to the south. There is an old camp-ground on the south end of the island, but as it is too much exposed to the wind we prefer a little bay behind a ledge of rock, where others have camped before. It is a quiet nook where we will be perfectly protected. Here is it our intention to remain for a few days.

The last bag of hardtack is getting low—not, we confess, to our regret, for all are getting tired of it, and long for other bread. After supper the cook begins making preparations for baking. He overhauls his stores for the package of pressed hops, but it is nowhere to be found. It has been forgotten. Well, it really does not much matter. He can easily find a substitute. A handful of moss is gathered from a neighbouring maple, and boiled as hops would be. The big tin dish is half filled with flour, and the boiling liquid strained into it. A yeast cake or two is reduced to powder, to which a handful of salt is added. This, with a portion of the flour, is mixed to the necessary consistency, when a couple of small sticks are laid across the top, and a clean towel is spread over all. It is now set on one side till next morning.

But as Canoe Lake, like all the others in this region, is famous both for the size and flavour of its trout, preparations are made to secure some. They are not to be had at this season either by angling from the shore or trawling, as the fish are deep down in the cold water beneath. Recourse must be had to the night line. One or two minnow hooks are soon obtained from some mysterious quarter, baited with a crumb of bread or a tiny piece of pork, and fishing for bait begins. As soon as caught it is placed in a pail of water to keep it alive—it would be labour thrown away to bait the hooks with lifeless material. The long trawling line we have brought is unwound, and hooks with two or three feet of line are attached to it at intervals of five or six feet. A favourable locality with twenty-five or thirty feet of water is selected. A half dozen pieces of dry cedar are made into floats. To each end of the trawling line another line, tied to a stone, is made fast, and also one of the floats with a sufficient length of line to keep the main one at least ten feet below the surface. All is now taken out in a canoe, and the end let down into the water. While one paddles slowly in the direction in which we wish the line to lie, another baits the hooks and pays out the line. At equal distances of about twenty feet the floats are attached till the whole is submerged.

The yeast is working splendidly, the cook informs us as we emerge from the tent next morning. He promises us a fresh loaf for dinner. While so saying he uncovers the dish, displaying the white frothy mass ready to overflow. With bared arms he quickly kneads it into dough; he then carefully smooths it over and lightly dusts it with dry flour, and replaces the cover. Our morning toilet is soon made, and in all the glory of clean guernsey or cotton shirt and socks, we sit down to breakfast.

But what about the night line? Has anyone been out to see? No, we will overhaul it after breakfast, and probably have fresh trout, as well as fresh bread, for dinner. One never thinks of any other fish than trout here. True, there are a few ling and lots of suckers, but if by any chance one is got on the line, it is contemptuously tossed back into the water.

It is a lovely morning; not a breath of air stirs. The surface of the lake is as smooth as a sheet of glass, and the sun looms with veiled face through a thin fleecy cloud that overhangs yonder pine-clad mountain. Perfect silence reigns, broken at short intervals only by the *ho-o-o* of a couple of loons sailing leisurely, gazing on the uncommon sight of our tent and the smoke of our fire in this unbroken wilderness. The floats on the night line are plainly in sight of the landing. One of them is twirling and shaking, and is slowly drawn down; in a couple of minutes the end again bobs up, topples over, and resumes its former position, to disappear yet again a moment afterwards. "There are fish on the line," is whispered. Instantly a canoe is launched and speeding off. The loons see it and down they go; we watch the spot, to see them rise again to the surface, for full five minutes. We then hear a distant *ho-o-o*. There they are, fully fifty rods away down the lake from where they disappeared.

By this time the canoe has reached the line, but as it is moving across our range of vision and also between us and the line, we can only conjecture that the men are unhooking the fish. In the course of a few minutes the prow is turned towards us, and the landing quickly reached. What beauties! A dozen at least! Look at the great big fellow with black back and grey sides! We have no means of weighing him, but he is two and one-half feet long at least, and of that peculiar kind of corpulency supposed to be characteristic of aldermen. There is another only a few inches shorter, but tapering in shape, and so beautifully spotted that it is only by the shape of his tail we know him to be a salmon and not a speckled trout; and here also is one of the genuine speckled trout of the lakes, fully a foot long and nearly half as much in depth. They are handed out to those on shore. Taking the pail of minnows on board, the men push off to the line to rebait the hooks. The fish are soon decapitated, split down the back, cleaned, and washed in the pure lake water. What rich-looking flesh! It is as red as any salt-water salmon!

The cook divides the fish into convenient-sized pieces for cooking, lightly sprinkles them over with salt, piles them on tin plates, and sets them away in a shaded corner ready for dinner. By the time this is done, his dough is ready for the next stage in its progress towards bread. A clean towel is spread out over a large piece of bark which has been laid on the ground for a bake board. A portion of the dough is cut off, firmly kneaded, and placed in the well-greased bake kettle; three more pieces of like size completely cover the bottom, and fill it halfway to the top. The pot-hole is scraped out, a shovelful of hot sand and coals thrown in. The bake kettle is carefully placed in position, a thin coating of cold ashes laid on top, and the whole completely covered with hot sand and coals so as to effectually prevent any escape of steam. A note is now taken of the time of day. An hour afterwards, the kettle is taken out and the lid removed. There is the rich brown top; it is full to the brim. A knife or sliver of wood is passed down through the centre. On being withdrawn it is found to be as clean as when put in. The big loaf is then turned out.

"It is as light as a feather," remarks the cook as he sets it on edge in the shade of an old stump to cool. In the course of a few minutes another is undergoing the same process.

A few of the boys have washing to do, and this is the next thing attended to. Then quietness reigns in camp till noon. By this time the second loaf is cooling by the side of the first. The grease produced from frying pork last night and this morning is emptied into the bake kettle, which is set on top of the fire; as soon as it arrives at the boiling point, the big lumps of fish are rolled in flour and laid in the bubbling mass. In half an hour we are enjoying dinner—and what a dinner! The bread is light and spongy, such as no cooking stove or bake oven could ever produce, and will keep for days without becoming either dry or hard; whilst more nutritious or richer-flavoured fish than our lake trout do not swim in any water, either fresh or salt.

CHAPTER 10 NOTES   *Restored by a day of rest and trout feasts on Canoe Lake, the Dickson party voyages northwards higher into the headwaters of the Oxtongue River (or Muskoka, as Dickson now calls it), into Joe and Tepee lakes. The stream flowing from Joe Lake down to Canoe has been largely flooded out by the raised water levels created by the Tea Lake and Joe Lake dams (the latter built originally in 1894); the modern canoe tripper will scarcely recognize Dickson's description.*

*Leaving part of the group to camp on Tepee Lake (considered part of Joe in Dickson's day), Dickson and the rest portage over into the Potter Creek valley and continue north, eventually crossing the height of land into the headwaters of the Petawawa River (Dickson coyly keeps its identity secret). The Tepee Lake campsite was the location of Dickson's store cache for his 1881 Hunter Township survey. The valley of Potter Creek, up through Potter and Brûlé lakes, was still remote, peaceful wilderness in the 1880s—tranquility shattered with the arrival of lumbermen and J.R. Booth's railway in the 1890s. A bustling village and sawmill later sprang up on the shore of Brûlé.*

*As noted in this chapter, extensive trapping was taking place on the Algonquin highlands in the late 19th century. Although this activity was banned when Algonquin Park was established, widespread poaching continued long afterwards. Many trappers in the Oxtongue headwaters were settlers from Parry Sound and Muskoka districts and Haliburton County to the west and southwest; selling furs supplemented the often meagre livelihood provided by pioneer farms on the Canadian Shield. Indian trappers had also operated in the region: Joe Lake was perhaps named for the Joe family from the Rama Reserve on Lake Couchiching.*

*Many of the portages used by Dickson are the same ones traversed by canoe trippers today—hardly surprising, since long use by Indians, trappers, and surveyors determined the easiest routes between lakes or around falls and rapids. Present-day travellers will also find themselves, in some cases, camping on sites originally chosen by Indians centuries ago. What made a site good then often makes it a good one now.*

## 10

## *About Trappers and Beavers*

————

IN CAMP ON THE LORD'S DAY WE DO NOT HEAR "THE SOUND OF THE church-going bell." There are sundry little jobs of work done that would never be thought of at home. The usual quiet of the day, however, is not altogether forgotten. Here and there solitary ones may be seen seated, perusing their pocket bibles, and the holy strains of sacred songs waft at intervals and in snatches across the quiet waters of the lake. We indulge in a ramble in the still, green woods, and a sail into the rock-bound, sand-fringed bay away to the northeast. A little before sunset we sup of the same luscious fare on which we dined. By the time darkness has fairly set in, all are in bed, refreshed and invigorated by the day's rest.

At intervals during the night the silence is broken by a long single cry, or howl, from the loons. At daybreak we are awakened by the howling of a pack of wolves up on the hills a short distance behind the camp. A few short, quick yelps are succeeded by a long dismal howl. Breakfast is soon despatched, the night line, with a dozen or so more fish, is taken in, and ere the rising sun dispels the light fleecy mist, we speed northwards across the smooth un-ruffled waters of the lake.

In a few minutes we are crossing the mouth of a little bay, into which a small creek empties its cool waters. There goes a round brown head with a small streak of dark brown fur behind it. We pause, gun in hand, ready for a shot should it come within reach. But in a moment we are discovered; up goes a black trowel-shaped object a few inches behind the streak of fur, then down it comes with a loud whack on the water. This act is of itself sufficient proof that the animal is a beaver taking his morning swim. The little animal never dives when alarmed without striking the water a smart stroke with its tail, making a noise that may be heard for at least a quarter of a mile.

Straight ahead, at the east end of a belt of sand, we see a large clump of tall, dark green alders. Towards this object we steer, for we know it marks the mouth of the river. In half an hour we are out of the lake. Here the Muskoka is no longer what might be strictly termed a river, but a mere creek, scarcely two rods wide, winding slowly by a tortuous course through a narrow alder and spruce swamp. Half a mile above the lake another and almost equally large creek [Potter] comes in from the west, which might easily be mistaken for the mainstream. We ply our paddles up the one to the right. It rapidly becomes shallow and narrow, and the numerous tree tops that obstruct the channel render our progress exceedingly slow. At last, after a mile or so, we reach another portage. To the right the water comes tumbling over a perpendicular fall of eight feet, and for the next half mile is one continuous rapid filled with fallen timber, till Big Joe Lake is reached. This is another favourite spot for trout fishing during high water.

The level, well-cleared portage is soon crossed, and we come to the foot of a long narrow bay stretching to the north. Immediately on the right hand is the outlet. The view towards the north is cut off by a high pine-clad hill. In a few minutes we are all afloat, picking our way through the mass of floodwood that has accumulated round the outlet. The bay is hemmed in between high pine-topped hills. On reaching its northern end, we find that the elevation that obstructed our view is an island, the larger part of the lake stretching away round it to the east. Our course lies along its west side. Straight ahead, a narrow gap runs between the mountains, with a larger opening beyond. Just after passing the north end of the island, a narrow opening is seen extending westerly up the side of the mountain. This line is the north boundary of Peck; we are now in the township of Hunter.

A few strokes more put us in a short, deep, narrow channel, and another lovely lake [Tepee] is before us, stretching away a mile and a quarter to the north. At its upper end a small mossy island almost conceals a long narrow neck of water. Should we follow this direction we would find a brook tumbling from a little beaver pond over a ledge of rock. Into the pond flows a muddy sluggish creek tenanted by countless bullfrogs, the croakings of which are almost deafening in the early months of spring—even now the cry of individual members is frequently heard. A quarter of a mile up the creek we would find Doe Lake [Littledoe], another beautiful sheet of water, spread out round numerous low, rocky, pine-clad points or extending into picturesque bays.

Should we wish to visit Bear Lake [Tom Thomson], we would turn to the left from Doe for half a mile up another wide marshy creek, the water almost completely concealed beneath a covering of water lilies; or, if we proceeded up the southeast bay, we would find a hunters' trail, pursuing which for ten minutes by the side of a brawling creek tossing and tumbling over its bed of gravel, we would arrive at the foot of short, narrow Hawk Lake [Bluejay]. Each one of those numerous lakes has been named, and every nook and corner in them explored and examined by the fur trapper, for each contains its quota of beaver, mink, otter, or muskrat, and their names have probably been suggested by the first animal or bird seen on their shores. Each when encountered seems more lovely than the last, displaying some new beauty of pine-covered bluff or rock-bound bay. As it is not our intention, however, to visit them at present, we steer for the west shore [of Tepee Lake], where a few charred and blackened balsams and cedars are seen.

We now reach another portage, and all are soon landed. We shall leave a portion of our party here for a day or two, while with the others we explore the country to the north. After dinner, the packs are quickly made up with the necessary supplies for our short absence. There is a special reason why we should not forget this spot. A few years ago, when engaged in a survey in this neighbourhood, we had our store camp here. It was found out by an enterprising bear. Several hundredweight of pork was carried off before his depredations were discovered, entailing on the whole party short rations.

Tossing packs and canoes on our shoulders, we wend our way into the woods. As there is a portage of a mile and a half to be crossed, we more than once throw the heavy packs on the ground and wipe big drops of perspiration from our flushed faces. After descending a mountainside we come to a large creek meandering through a bed of big stones. This is the same stream [Potter Creek] we passed in the morning a little above Canoe Lake. It is crossed by stepping from stone to stone. Threading our way for a few rods up its west bank, we arrive at the foot of Potter's Lake. Only a narrow neck of water is visible from where we stand, but as we glide over a surface ruffled slightly by a light northern breeze, its beautiful bays and points are one after another approached and passed. We lay our course for its most northwesterly bay. Past a solitary rock, rising like a lone sentinel out of the water, we pass several small islets, and see a few beaver houses on the shores. The canoe is drawn out beneath the spreading boughs of an overhanging cedar a few rods to the south of where another good-sized creek empties in.

Again we shoulder our traps, for a distance of thirty chains by the side of a creek flowing down a rocky gorge. It is perceptibly smaller than the stream below Potter's Lake, for we are nearing its headwaters. This brings us to the foot of Burnt Lake [Brûlé], another small gem, scarcely a mile in length. We cross to its northern end. A small rivulet a couple of yards wide meanders through an opening in a ledge of rock. Stepping on shore and shouldering the packs, in less than five minutes we reach another small sheet of water [Rosswood Lake] extending a quarter of a mile to the east. Across its outlet, and completely stopping up the creek, stretches an embankment of earth, stones, limbs of trees, and short junks of wood. It seems a mass of matter thrown accidentally together, forming a narrow ridge on top, over which the water trickles. On the lower side it is perpendicular, ends of limbs and timber sticking confusedly out, while on the upper side it presents a smooth surface of gravel and black mud extending by a gentle slope away into the bottom of the pond. This is a beaver dam, built by the little animals to raise the water of the small lake a sufficient height to preserve the winter supply of food beneath the surface.

The beaver does not always select a lake for its home. More frequently he pitches on a small creek flowing through a swamp, and builds a dam from four to six, sometimes as much as eight feet high across the lower end to the high land on either side. Then the beaver house, shaped like a large cock of hay, is constructed some distance above the dam. By instinct the creatures seem to know how high the water will reach, and the house is made high enough to be four or five feet above the surface of the water. The entrance is near the bottom, while near the top and just above the highest water level, a dry, warm chamber is left; in this undisturbed home they pass the long winter and bring forth their young. Gradually the water rises till it reaches the top of the dam, when the surplus overflows in tiny little drippings. The beavers collect a large quantity of their favourite food and deposit it in a pile by the side of the house for the winter supply. The trapper is careful not to cut away the dam—if he does, the family will at once decamp for "fresh fields and pastures new." But a small cut is made in the top. By the side of this the trap is set a few inches underneath the water and made fast by a chain, a few feet long, to a stout picket driven into the bottom a few feet farther out in the water. More frequently, it is attached to what is termed a tally pole—a thick pole of dry light wood six or eight feet long with the trap chain made fast to the centre of it—which is left floating.

The trapper is careful to leave as few traces of his presence as possible, and if the whole can be done without his getting out of his canoe at all, so much the better, for the beaver has a very acute sense of smell. The quick instinct of the animal very soon detects the slightest variations in the height of the water. During the night an examination is made in order to find out the cause. As soon as the cut is discovered they at once set to work to repair the damage. Ere long one of them gets a foot caught in the iron grasps of the trap; he then dashes off for his only harbour of refuge, the deep water, and speedily drowns. If the trap has been made fast to a picket stuck in the bottom, the game is bagged as soon as the pond is visited; but if it has been fastened to a tally pole, it may be found in any part of the pond, for the beaver will live for a considerable time under water, swimming round till dead, dragging the pole along with him. This is usually made heavy enough to float both beaver and trap, and is easily discovered. Not only is the beaver valuable for his fur, but his flesh is held in high esteem, the tail especially being a rare delicacy.

The areas of the ponds which have thus been formed vary in size from an acre or so in extent to several hundred acres, and the timber, being constantly under water, dies in a few years, falls down, and in course of time completely decays. What was once a thick swamp is now an open lake, with here and there the naked white trunk of an extra-large tamarack or cedar standing. But trappers arrive on the scene. If they are Indians, and there is no danger of white men coming in to dispute the trapping ground, only a few of the beavers will be taken each year. The dam is left intact, so as not to frighten the rest of the family or families; since beavers breed rapidly, a large increase may be depended upon each succeeding year.

If the trappers are white men, a very different course is pursued: the animals, if possible, are completely cleaned out. A large gap is cut in the dam so that the game may be more easily captured; or, if this is not done, the embankment will in the course of a few years get out of repair, causing leaks, when the pond will gradually dry up. In a few more years it will be found completely covered with a luxuriant growth of tall grass, and become what is called a beaver meadow. The grass, known as blue joint, is cut in large quantities in autumn by the lumbermen, who put it up in stacks for horse and ox feed in the shanties during winter. If properly cured in season, and lightly sprinkled with salt when being stacked, it is considered little inferior to the best timothy hay.

This whole section of country is hunted over by an army of trappers during October and November, and again in March and April. The hunt is made singly and in couples. Each has his own trapping ground, and by a code of laws peculiar to themselves no one ever trespasses upon the limits of his neighbour. Before commencing operations, an examination of the section selected has been carefully made, and all the signs of the different kinds of fur-bearing animals noted. A rude camp is constructed on the shore of some lake or river, near the centre of the limits. The space is then gone over, the various kinds of traps set for the amphibious animals, while a line of deadfalls is also constructed through the woods, in various directions away from the waters, for fisher and marten, and perhaps an additional one or two for bears.

The trapper calculates on visiting his traps at least once a week to secure the game and reset the trap or deadfall. In some sections he can do this and return to camp each night. In others the extent of territory is too large, or the lakes and streams so located, that he cannot get over the ground so expeditiously; in this case he has a number of camps located at convenient distances, in which he spends nights alternately, collecting the fur as he proceeds, which he brings to the central or store camp. The fur-bearing animals are all the trapper attempts to take. Only a sufficient number of deer are killed to supply the camp with venison, and probably a few moose for the sake of their skins and massive antlers, the whole carcass of rich juicy meat being left to rot, or to feed the wolves. As soon as the ice begins to form in the fall, or before it breaks up in the spring, the hunters return to the settlement with their load of valuable furs.

But while discussing the habits of the beaver and his natural enemy—his only enemy, we might say—the sun has been gradually but steadily declining in the west, and we are yet a considerable distance from where we propose to camp for the night. In a brief space of time we are across the little pond and speeding over a narrow portage to the northeast. In half an hour we find ourselves on the shore of another little lake [Straight Shore], with its small outlet immediately to the right of the end of the portage. Here again we embark. No one ever thinks of walking round any of these sheets of water, no matter how small, and we carry the canoes and make them carry us alternately. At the end of half a mile we arrive on the shore of McIntosh Lake. It is a lovely sheet of water studded with naked rocks and small, rocky, pine-clad islets. Immense pines overhang the water and crown the rocks on its eastern shore, while its western hills are clothed in a dense growth of black birch and maple, with a fringe of cedar, hemlock, and alder round the shore. Here there is no stream emptying to the south or west, but a large creek winds in through an extensive tamarack swamp from the south. In the northeast a valley of alders extends easterly between the mountains, with a quantity of white driftwood piled up against the shore denoting the outlet.

The ridge we have just crossed between this and the last lake is the height of land, and for the present we are done with the Muskoka; the waters we now gaze upon find their way to the ocean through the valley of the Ottawa. We paddle straight into the head of a deep bay almost due north from the end of the trail, and pitch our camp for the night.

The mists engendered by the cool night still hang heavily on the water when our camp is struck. A short half mile through a lovely hardwood glade brings us to Wolf Lake [Timberwolf], a sheet of pure limpid water. Proceeding for a mile or so across the mouths of the small narrow bays that indent its eastern shore, a V-shaped bay is before us, extending to the northeast; arriving at its foot, we enter the outlet, a creek with just water enough to float the canoes. We proceed down its winding course, cross a beaver meadow covered with a luxuriant growth of blue joint, pass through a narrow opening in an old beaver dam, and in another hour are in Misty Lake. Extending away to the west between high hardwood hills, it is dotted here and there with small islands. Away at the distance of a mile we see two objects moving steadily towards the north shore. Are they loons, or what? The field glass is brought to bear upon them—an old cow moose and her calf. The flesh of the calf would be a rare delicacy, but they are too far away for us to overtake them, and long ere we could come within shot they would be far into the deep woods where pursuit would be hopeless.

We make our way towards the northeast, and rounding a point, pass through a short shallow narrows a chain or so wide, when we find the water again expands into a broad lake stretching away a mile and a half to the east. An open and recently cut line on the

narrow neck of land south of the narrows is the boundary between the townships of Hunter and Devine. Proceeding easterly
to the foot of the lake, here a narrow neck extends still farther a
little to the south of east, till finally the outlet is reached. Here a
stream at least four times the size of the Muskoka above Canoe
Lake rushes away to the east over a bed of huge boulders. There is
a well-cut portage on the south shore. We land and follow it a
quarter of a mile, when it ends by the side of smooth, deep, rapid
stream. We have discovered another river. What is its name? Let us
retrace our way to Joe Lake and endeavour to find it again, at a
point lower down and by another route.

We must try to rejoin this evening the camp we left yesterday
on Joe Lake, or go supperless to bed. While seated by the shore of
the newly found river we had eaten our last crust. Lake and portage are each in succession passed as rapidly as possible. The sun is
nearly set by the time we arrive at the head of Potter's Lake, and
total darkness has set in before we step on shore at the outlet. It is
only a mile and a half to camp; but a mile and a half over a rough
and hilly portage, bending beneath a canoe or pack on a dark
night, is rather more than we care to undertake. A big fire is soon
blazing up, by the light of which we fell a few small balsams. The
night is clear and calm, with no signs of rain, and the dense foliage
of the trees will effectually keep off the heavy dew, so we shall dispense with the tent, by which we avoid an extra half hour of work
in the darkness. As a substitute for supper, an extra pipe is smoked,
after which each one spreads down a few balsam boughs as he
chooses, and wrapping himself in his blanket, tired Nature claims
her rights. In a few minutes all are sound asleep.

CHAPTER II NOTES    *The canoe route leading up through Joe and Burnt Island lakes, then down though the Otterslides, is now part of one of the most heavily travelled in Algonquin. In this chapter, however, Dickson sees not another soul as he paddles the same waters—which would certainly not happen today in midsummer!*

*Raised water levels behind the Joe Lake Dam have resulted in some changes since Dickson's account. The "shallow tortuous creek" between Joe and Little Joe is now a strait, and the lower reaches of the creek flowing into the head of Little Joe are flooded out.*

*Burnt Island Lake, largest in the Oxtongue (Muskoka) headwaters, was named in 1853 by geologist Alexander Murray (who also named Lake of Bays, Oxtongue, Canoe, and Otterslide lakes), but for many years it was simply called Island Lake. Names of many Algonquin lakes were changed or revised in the 1930s to clear up confusion. Dickson surveyed Burnt Island during the McLaughlin Township survey in 1883.*

*Dickson frequently refers to the hills on the Algonquin highlands as "mountains." They did begin as mountains, but worn down over the ages, they are now properly described as hills. In the territory Dickson passed through, local relief generally ranges from 30 to 90 metres (100 to 300 feet), with the occasional hill somewhat higher. The mountain towering "high above its fellows" north of Burnt Island Lake on page 140 is Trout Mountain. One of the higher summits in Algonquin Park, it stands more than 150 metres (500 feet) above Trout Lake to the north. A fire lookout tower was constructed on it in 1922.*

*Often mentioned in the book are large accumulations of driftwood at the outlets of lakes. Drawn by the current, the material inevitably piled up at these locations and provided a reliable beacon for the traveller attempting to locate the outflowing stream among a sometimes confusing profusion of similar-looking bays.*

*In this chapter, Jack, the "best hunter," misses again—was Dickson poking fun at some boastful member of one of his survey crews? A deer finally is successfully shot, but Jack isn't specifically given credit.*

## 11

## *Incidents by Flood and Field*

THE FIRST RAYS OF THE MORNING SUN HAVE NOT BEGUN TO GILD THE tops of the tallest pines when all are awake and on their feet. Ten minutes later we are wending our way along the narrow portage. It does not take long for us to reach the camp, and with a loud cheer we awaken our comrades from their morning nap. While breakfast of steaming beans and newly caught trout is being prepared, we indulge in a refreshing plunge in the crystal waters of the lake. A hearty breakfast is soon partaken of, and word passed round to strike camp and pack up.

In less than another hour everything is done up, the canoes are loaded, and once more we are off. In a few minutes we are through the narrows and speeding east between the north shore of Joe Lake and the island. A mile to the east, a small spot of tall beaver grass marks the inlet. Just before reaching it we discover, through a grove of alders on our left, a small pond in a beaver meadow. Pausing to have a look at it, we notice an antlered buck feeding on the far shore. Our hunter is quickly set on land. He creeps stealthily to the thin grove of alders, found to be growing on top of an old beaver dam. It is a long shot, but the deer may step into the woods at any moment, and taking a hasty aim, he fires. The antlered head instantly rises high in air, the eyes turn towards us, and the small column of smoke is discovered, denoting the presence of an enemy. He sharply wheels round, his white tail rises, and with a single bound he is out of sight. The bullet has passed over his back, for Jack informs us that he overestimated the distance and sighted the rifle too high.

We are now in a shallow tortuous creek with scarcely enough water to float our light canoes. In less than ten minutes we reach Little Joe Lake. Half a mile straight ahead is a grass- and alder-covered marsh. To the left, the shore is comparatively low and timbered with pine and hemlock, while on the right rises a high mountain covered with hardwood. Soon the edge of the marsh is reached, through a bed of water lilies out of which half a dozen ducks have risen. They fly right round the lake, gradually attaining a higher elevation, then pass swiftly overhead, speeding towards the west.

The Muskoka River is now only a few feet wide, and the canoes must ascend it in Indian file. In a few minutes we are sailing along a narrow crooked lane between overhanging alders. Frequently we have to duck the head to escape the interlaced limbs, and occasionally we must cut a newly fallen balsam out of the way. In about an hour we arrive at a portage on the south side, and must land. About this, the alders hang so thick and low over the water that it is impossible to force even a small canoe through them. We have now reached the head of canoe navigation on the Muskoka River. True, it is still a few miles to the fountainhead, but we shall make the distance by lakes, as the stream itself is no longer navigable.

Portaging a quarter of a mile through a thick grove of tall pines, we make the shore of a little pond. Hastily loading up, in five minutes we are across it. It is on the creek, for there is the outlet to the left where it rushes through a mass of boulders, while to the right a small cataract tumbles into it over a ledge of rock. Climbing another rough portage of ten or twelve rods, we reach a long narrow pond [Baby Joe Lake] nestling between high pine-capped hills and stretching away for half a mile to the north. Two-thirds of the way up, a small fern-clad island nestles close to the east shore. When nearing the upper end the ear is once more greeted with the noise of falling water. Picking our way for a couple of chains amongst the stones in the little brook, there on our right are the first falls of the Muskoka, counting from what may be fairly termed its source. At the end of another short rough portage, about the same length as the last, a small sheet of water stretches before the eye, extending apparently about half a mile eastwards. We are now on the shore of Island Lake, and shall dine before re-embarking.

A ten-minute pull brings us to the eastern end of the water visible from the landing, when, rounding a rock, we enter a narrow neck of water, and a few strokes of the paddle carry us through. There before us is Island Lake, stretching away to the northeast. On the north stands a towering mountain clothed to the summit with tall graceful red pine; and on the south, a magnificent ridge of high hardwood land. Away at a distance of a mile and a quarter to the east the view is cut off by a cluster of small islands and a high and heavily timbered rocky point jutting out from the south, while a deep bay extends away to the southeast. On our right an open lane in the woods running south marks the east boundary of the township of Hunter. We are now in the township of McLaughlin.

We skim lightly across the deep blue waters, assisted by a light southwestern breeze, and in half an hour are passing through the cluster of small islands seen from the narrows. Here another bay extends about half a mile to the north; and here again we pass through a narrow neck of water. The main body of the lake lies before the eye, stretching at least four miles to the northeast. To the southeast lies another deep bay, into which empty the waters of Linda's Lake, embosomed between high hardwood hills three miles to the south. Away in the far east we can see a high mountain clothed in maple and birch, a few miles beyond which, we are told, lie the great Opeongo Lakes.

Numerous picturesque bays indent the shore on either side. While still a mile from the east end we turn to the left round a low rocky point, and pass between the shore and a long narrow island. On our left another bay stretches nearly a mile and a half to the north. At its head is a swamp through which a creek winds its way from a valley between the mountains in the background. Follow it up and you will find, at the distance of a mile or two, its origin in a small marsh or beaver meadow, and you will have reached the fountainhead—the source of the great Muskoka River. Away still farther north a mountain towers high above its fellows, clothed in hardwood timber with a few green pines stretching sentinel-like over all.

Before us on the main shore, and south of this bay, are a few acres of land that have been burnt over, now clothed with a dense growth of small poplar and cherry. Towards the east end of this we lay our course. But before we can touch shore our little vessels ground on a bed of yellow sand. We carry the loads on shore, then lift the canoes out of the waters that go to swell the volume of Lake Huron. When they are again launched it will be on a tributary of the Ottawa.

The sun is still high. We conclude to cross the portage, and if we can make no further progress, camp for the night at the other end. We have scarcely gone half a mile up and down a few knolls through the thick woods in a northeasterly direction, when we see other water glimmering through the trees. It looks like a pond extending just a short distance to the east. We cannot tell whether, on the whole, we have ascended or descended from Island Lake, for we seem to have travelled as much downhill as up, and have also passed a few narrow necks of swamp. The two waters have apparently about the same level. But this narrow elevation here forms the dividing ridge between the waters of Lake Huron and the Ottawa River.

Scattered round at the north end of the portage are a few leg bones, ribs, and vertebræ of a moose. By the time everything has been got across, our usual hour for camping has arrived. All hands immediately set to work in getting up tents and doing all the other odd jobs of camping time.

Another lovely morning. As usual, we are up with the lark and soon speeding across the pure limpid water. Emerging from the small pond-like bay, we enter a broad sheet of water extending nearly a mile to the east. Nearing the bottom, we see that it spreads away towards the north. We steer round a point and keep along its west shore, heading towards a naked rock at the north. When about halfway across, we pass a large island on our right hand, the main body of the lake extending to the east behind it. This sheet of water is Little Otter Slide Lake. In a few minutes we reach the outlet. The trunks of two or three large pines have fallen across the stream. Stooping under one, lifting over another, and cutting the end off a third, we finally enter a broad, shallow, muddy creek with a scarcely perceptible current. To the right is a high mountain, thickly timbered with large pines and hemlocks right down to the water's edge. On the left is a large spruce swamp backed by a high hardwood hill in the distance.

The stream is so shallow that every stroke of the paddle turns up soft black slimy mud, and in several spots the canoes can only with difficulty be forced through it. We dare not step out, for if we did we would be engulfed in the spongy mass. In half an hour we enter another large lake. We are almost at the west shore, and it extends in a broad sheet away to the east. Straight ahead, at a distance of a mile, a pile of driftwood marks the outlet. The south shore is a high hardwood bluff, while pine- and hemlock-capped mountains encircle the north side. The greater part of the lake lies completely hidden behind a large island and a cluster of smaller ones. Unless we go east beyond those we shall only have the pleasure of gazing upon a very small portion of Otter Slide Lake.

The landing, immediately to the west of the head of the creek, is soon reached, and we repeat the same old process of taking out, packing up, crossing, and loading up again, that we have become so well accustomed to. The portage this time is almost perfectly level, well cut out, and scarcely a five-minute walk, when we are again afloat in a tiny pond, guiding the canoes past stones and round sunken timbers. Another somewhat longer, and decidedly rougher, portage has to be overcome, and we emerge on the creek at the foot of a shallow stony rapid. The stream is not sufficiently wide for two canoes to go abreast. By this time the cravings of the inner man have again warned us that the dinner hour ought to be near. The pail of hot tea is quickly prepared, and each with his chunk of bread and pork is busily engaged. An hour later finds us paddling slowly down the gently flowing stream. It is in many spots so shallow that there is scarcely water enough to float us, and as we pursue its windings we steer towards nearly every point on the compass. It runs through a wide marsh dotted with clusters of alders, balsam, and spruce, nearly the whole surface being covered with tall beaver grass. At short intervals we pass over deep pools, and peering into the water we see a fine trout dart from underneath a projecting alder.

Suddenly the echoes are awakened by the report of a gun. What have the lads got this time? We round a sharp bend. There the canoe lies with its end drawn up on a muddy bank, but there are no men to be seen. We pause and look round, when suddenly, a few rods off, they rise to their feet by the side of a clump of alders and advance, dragging with them a fine fat yearling buck, its head adorned with a small neat pair of velvet-covered horns. A single drop of blood behind the shoulder marks the spot where he received his death wound. Mutual congratulations are exchanged; we shall now, in addition to fresh trout, enjoy the luxury of fresh venison. The game is laid on its back, ripped open, and the entrails removed; the head is also cut off, for we carry no useless weight, and left alongside the other refuse as food for the ravens, which are croaking overhead and perched on the limbs of a neighbouring tree.

There is a slight shifting of cargoes to make room for the venison, and again we get under way. We now enter another small pond, or expansion of the creek, a couple of chains wide by twice as many long. At its foot is an old dilapidated beaver dam. A low murmuring of water below announces the presence of another rapid. To the left is the end of the portage, and one canoe, suddenly fired with the ambition to reach the landing first, dashes off ahead of the others; but scarcely has it got fairly under way when it strikes against the sharp top of a sunken stone. A big hole cut clean through the bark is the consequence, and the water rushes in. Ere they can make the landing and disembark, the bottom of the packs are submerged. A tiny stream of water pours from each as they are lifted out. Half the contents are thoroughly soaked. This is the first serious damage any of our little fleet has sustained. The canoe is turned up for examination. There it is, a large ragged hole, with the torn bark doubled in against the ribs. It is carefully smoothed out again, and the torn edges brought together. A piece of strong grey cotton, perhaps twice as large as the rent, is got ready, and the gum melted to its thinnest capacity. The cotton is put in and thoroughly saturated with the gum, when it is taken and smoothly spread over the hole, the greatest care being observed that the edges are well smoothed down. In a few minutes it is dry and cold, and the canoe as sound as ever.

Halfway across the portage we find the stump of a large pine that has been cut with an axe. The body of the tree has been taken away, but in the place where it lay, a number of slabs and a large quantity of chips bear unmistakable evidence that it has been made into a stick of square timber. We are again in the track of the lumbermen. The last we saw was on the portage between Lake of Bays and Hunter's Bridge. This is of itself sufficient evidence that we are on other than Muskoka waters: the creek we are threading must be a tributary of the Madawaska or the Petewawa River.

We are in a little while again afloat, moving noiselessly down the narrow creek. The ease with which the canoe is propelled is a pleasant change from the steady strong stroke which had to be constantly maintained while ascending against the current. But it has been gradually clouding up ever since nine o'clock, and now heavy drops begin to fall. They soon thicken into a steady rain. The light rubber sheets, which have been kept ready for such an emergency, are quickly spread over the loads. In half an hour we reach a short shallow spot where, though it can scarcely be called a rapid, the stream is almost completely filled with big stones, and we will require to make a short portage. As the rain has been steadily increasing, with every indication of a wet evening, we conclude that our best course is to camp for the night.

The canoes are quickly unloaded and inverted over their cargoes. All is hurry and despatch now. Not only will the goods get wet, but we will soon be drenched ourselves. In a few minutes the tent is up, the floor made as level as possible. The balsam brush is picked and laid in place. Though dripping wet, no water ever penetrates the short green spines; a single shake releases it of all that clings to it, and when spread down it is as thoroughly dry as if there had been no rain at all. A large fire is soon blazing near the door of the tent, and a tumpline stretched along the ridgepole is loaded with wet clothes hung up to dry. The rain gives us little annoyance. We knew before starting that there were discomforts in camping we would have to bear with, that we need not expect to make our trip without being occasionally caught in a shower and probably getting a thorough wetting, so that little inconvenience is borne without a grumble.

We will have fresh venison for supper, and in due time a part of the carcass is stripped of its hide. The heart and liver of the animal are preserved. The bake kettle is nearly filled with rich juicy steaks and a few slices of fat pork. What a supper we do make! By the time we have had enough of the luxurious morsels there is no room left for either apple sauce or rice. After supper two of the party take a canoe down the brook a short distance to a deep pool to angle for trout, for contrary to expectation the rain has entirely ceased and the sun shines out at short intervals through rents in the parting clouds. But they speedily return, literally chased from their fishing ground by myriad sandflies and mosquitoes, which they say no man could withstand.

Every wet article is now got out and spread before the blazing fire, and by the time the night has fairly set in, all is once more thoroughly dry. A bright starlight night with countless hosts of fireflies succeeds the wet afternoon, but the sandflies are so annoying that a smudge has to be kept going in the back of the tent till long past midnight.

CHAPTER 12 NOTES    *Several good-sized lakes in the heart of Algonquin Park collect the inflow from the upper tributaries of the Petawawa
(including Otterslide Creek, which Dickson is still descending as this
chapter opens) before the river tumbles northeasterly off the Algonquin
highlands. From a campsite on Big Trout Lake, the party will explore
these picturesque lakes for a few days. Much of the countryside described
in this chapter lies in Bishop Township, surveyed in 1884. Dickson first
visited Big Trout and Trout lakes (then known as White Trout and Little
White Trout) in 1883 during his survey of McLaughlin Township.*

*Of interest here is evidence again of the activities of the lumbermen,
still entirely absent in the adjacent headwaters of the Oxtongue River in
the 1880s. Now, lumber shanties, haul roads, a dam and a bridge, and
evidence of cutting are all observed—but no actual activity, of course,
since in that era cutting took place in the winter, the logs were floated
downstream out of the wilderness in the spring, and in summer, peace
and silence reigned. Lumbermen had been working their way up the
Petawawa River since before 1830. Some years prior to Dickson's survey,
they reached the Trout lakes area and took out the very best and largest
pine for both square timber and sawlogs. In his report on Bishop Township Dickson also mentions current activity (in season) by the McLachlin
Brothers of Arnprior. Within a decade, lumbermen would be swarming
over the entire upper Petawawa watershed, meeting up with companies
that had finally advanced to the height of land on the Georgian Bay
side. (Logging began later on the westward-flowing Georgian Bay rivers.)*

*In his survey report Dickson credits the McLachlin Brothers with
building the new dam described on Big Trout Lake. Possibly there had
been an older lumbering dam on the site: flooding from that might
explain the dead trees noted in the large marsh (Grassy Bay) at the
upper end of Trout Lake. The McLachlin Brothers later established a
substantial depot farm on the north shore of Trout.* (Note: on the map
Canoe Routes of Algonquin Provincial Park, *Trout Lake is now
shown as White Trout.)*

## 12

## *We Continue Our Explorations*

———◼ ◼———

A HEAVY VEIL OF MIST ENSHROUDS BOTH MARSH AND STREAM, HANG-
ing also in thick masses in the dense woods of the swamp, as we
emerge from the tent in the early morning. A mile or more of
what may very properly be termed narrow navigation brings us to
the head of a long portage. The stream is still more winding than
we found it yesterday. At one point we speed over a deep clear
stretch; then, with heads stooped to avoid the overhanging alders,
we wind round a sharp bend; at several points logs must be circumvented or cut out of the way; then again we float beneath an
arch of boughs that completely veils the stream, till finally we
bring up at the portage on the left bank. Bending beneath our
loads, we are off down the shore of the creek. In a few minutes
the path crosses the stream. We get over on a fallen tree, though
some of the party who could not walk the slippery log must wade
the stream. They get wet feet, but what of it? So long as the water
is warm they do not care. As soon as the portage is passed, the wet
socks can be replaced by dry ones, and one rarely catches cold in
camp. This is the longest portage since we crossed the height of
land, but after crossing the creek it follows an old lumber road,
making the travelling much easier, though it is some five-eighths
of a mile long. The packs are finally laid down by the side of still
water in another little alder marsh.

Less than five minutes farther in the canoes we reach yet another landing. It is not merely the end of a portage this time, for here is a small cleared space covered not with wild grass, but by clover and timothy hay, and the trough roof of an old lumber shanty is also visible. Stepping up the bank, we see, a few rods off, the big old building of rough unhewn logs notched into each other at the corners, and roofed over with split logs slightly hollowed out to carry off the rain and melted snow. A small frame of slabs rises four feet from the centre of the roof: this is the chimney, the big camboose being directly beneath it. The entrance is by a small door three by four feet in the centre of one end; a few panes of glass halfway down one side serve for a window.

The building is at least thirty by forty feet, and seven or eight in height. It must have been built a good time ago: the dilapidated condition of the adjacent stables bears testimony that it is a number of years since is was used. But as the interior of the shanty is now filled with provisions for both man and beast, it is evidently the intention of the owners to reoccupy it next winter. The construction of roads is so expensive in this unbroken wilderness that the owner of timber limits finds it cheaper and more convenient, before the ice in the lakes and streams breaks up in the spring and the smooth winter roads have become impassible, to lay in a sufficient supply of provisions to last his gang of men—usually sent into the woods about the end of autumn—till the ice has again taken and the snows of early winter render the roads passable.

A few men are generally left in charge during the summer to raise vegetables at some central point known as the farm or depot. At short intervals they visit all the shanties, where provisions, sleighs, and such like have been stored, to see that everything is safe, that none have been broken into nor an attack made upon the provisions by bears, and also that no fires have been started in the woods. In this instance the door of the shanty is firmly barricaded and chained up, and the chimney covered with heavy timbers, to resist the attacks of Mr. Bruin. On going round to the side of the building we see a small excavation where one of those gentlemen attempted to dig his way in beneath the foundation, but had to relinquish the task and forgo the pleasure of dining on salt pork.

The obstructions in the creek have become so numerous, and have occasioned so many delays, that we have only made a short distance this morning. When everything is on shore by the side of the old shanty, it is time to prepare dinner. We hear the noise of a fall behind the building. While the cook prepares the tea and fries a venison steak, a fishing line and rod are fitted up, and we make our way down a narrow path to the side of the stream. Here, at the foot of a beautiful cascade, it is spanned by the remains of a rude bridge. A rough lumber road winds up the opposite bank. Immediately beneath the bridge is a deep pool, and here there ought to be some brook trout. The hook is quickly baited and thrown in. It is scarcely ten seconds out of sight when there is a succession of sharp, strong tugs, and a big white fish, at least a foot long, is the next moment floundering on the shore. We pick it up and examine it. It is entirely covered with large white scales. This is no trout, but the chub of the Ottawa waters. A considerable quantity of chub are to be had in the Muskoka waters, but there they are always small, scarcely larger than a good-sized minnow. Here they are as large as the biggest speckled trout and found in almost unlimited numbers.

Before either the pork or venison is cooked, we return to the camp with a half dozen large fish, which in a very few minutes are dressed and added to the pan. The bright noonday sun is intensely hot, and each with a plate of steaming meat, large slice of bread, and dish of scalding-hot tea, seeks a shady nook in which to discuss his meal.

The stream below the shanty is still small, having nothing but a few small rivulets to swell its water below Otter Slide Lake. Again we trace its winding course through an alder marsh. There are high dark woods on either side, but straight downstream an open space gradually increases in size. In half an hour, passing through a narrow opening in a bed of rushes, we suddenly find ourselves in open water. Beautiful White Trout Lake [Big Trout] spreads before the eye, and our canoes rise and fall on the heavy groundswell.

A stiff western breeze is blowing, raising a heavy sea that is too much for our light canoes, so we steer along the west shore and find it all we can do to cross the mouths of a couple of small bays. As we slowly proceed, the lake gradually unfolds to view, stretching away to the north and east. Coasting along the shore, we pass the end of an open line leading westerly. This is the northern boundary of the township of McLaughlin, and we now enter the township of Bishop. Half an hour after entering the lake, we reach a rocky point where the shore trends sharply to the west. Here we must stop, for the canoes could not live for five minutes in the long white-capped rollers that thunder by, chasing each other in rapid succession.

In a few minutes everything is disembarked and laid out on top of the bank. It is a lovely spot for a camp, commanding one of the best views on the whole lake. The field glass is quickly adjusted and brought to bear successively all round. A deep bay, thickly indented with smaller ones, extends for upwards of a mile to the west. Right in front and to the northwest, a cluster of small pine-topped islands obstructs the view in that direction. Beyond their east end a part of the west shore is seen, on which a narrow strip of small poplar is evidence of its having been burnt over a few years ago. This extends northerly to near the outlet, which is concealed by an island densely clothed with the same variety of young timber.

On the east side of the outlet, and extending away inland, is a high hardwood mountain with a margin of pine and other evergreens encircling the waters. Right north of us the mountain slopes down to the water's edge a mile and a half distant, where stands a recently erected lumber shanty. A deep bottle-shaped bay stretches away to the northeast and rounds up to another hardwood hill a quarter of a mile southeast of the shanty. From this a bay extends far away eastward, its end concealed behind still another cape. The remainder of the lake bends again in a graceful curve away to the east, and finally winds up by a regular sweep to the mouth of the creek we have just descended. The whole shore is covered by a dense primeval forest of hardwood and evergreens. The scenery during the latter part of October, when the green foliage has assumed its autumn colouring, must be gorgeous beyond conception.

Heavy masses of dark clouds drift athwart the heavens, emitting at short intervals light squalls of rain, while away on the east shore the swell breaks in clouds of spray at least twenty feet high on the boulder-strewn beach. The tents are soon set up, extra care being bestowed on the beds to have them level and soft, as we are likely to remain here for a few days, and a number of balsam tops are dragged forward and piled up to windward of the camp to break the force of the gale. Another dozen or so of the big white chub were caught as we descended the last part of the creek, and the little sheltered bay in which we landed contributed as many more, so there is a bake-kettleful of fried fish for supper. They have not the delicious tender flavour of the trout, and there are sundry small bones distributed promiscuously through the flesh, but still they are good wholesome food, and are most thoroughly enjoyed.

Now at the close of another week, we are well pleased to have arrived at such a pleasant spot in which to spend the Sabbath. The instructions of the Fourth Commandment are not very strictly adhered to: the day is spent in a manner somewhat similar to the last. There is more clothes-washing and, in addition, considerable more mending done, for this packing over rough portages is very trying on our dry goods as well as the feet wear.

Shortly after dinner the cook is observed to be engaged in some mysterious operations by the side of the bake kettle. A little water has been put in the bottom, which is then covered with slices of fat pork. On top of this a layer of little flat lumps of dough is placed, then another of square chunks of venison. More pieces of dough and venison are placed side by side till the kettle is filled, and a thin crust of dough is laid completely over all. He now sets it in the pot-hole and covers it over with hot sand and coals. Next, a big roly-poly pudding of dried apples and raisins is sewed up in a clean cotton cloth and placed in the largest pail, which has been half filled with water, and then hung over the fire. By six o'clock both the contents of the pail and bake kettle are cooked, and we sit down to a supper fit for a king.

It is another glorious morning. The wind has entirely gone down and the surface of the lake is as smooth as a mirror. The high winds of the two preceding days seem to have completely dispelled the damp and mist occasioned by the recent rain, and the atmosphere has now a peculiar clearness but rarely seen. We purpose today exploring the west part of the lake, into which, we have learned, the waters of Misty Lake empty. The camp is left in charge of the cook, and taking with us a light lunch, an early start is made. We always prefer an early start in the morning, when the air is cool and fresh. We thread our way through the group of islands to the northwest of the camp, and steer across the mouth of another bay, now for the first time discovered, extending away to the west. Past a few more little islets, right in front is a beautiful birch point, on the north of which we now discover another picturesque birch-fringed bay. A high hardwood mountain rises on the left; as we skirt its base up the bay, it gradually closes in till at last the lake is merely a narrow neck of water scarcely a chain in width. A few strokes of the paddle suffice to speed us through the short narrows, and we enter what the trappers call Little White Trout Lake [Trout Lake], stretching away to the west for upwards of two miles.

Numerous small birch- and pine-fringed points protrude from the north shore, while on the south a bold burnt bluff at least three hundred feet high towers above the water. High up near the top a bald-headed eagle rises from her nest on a narrow project- ing ledge. We paddle sharply for half an hour along its base, then the shore turns suddenly to the southeast. Right opposite the rocky point round which we steer, at a distance of three-eighths of a mile, is another low point clothed in dark green pines, maple, and hemlock. To the south of it lies a lovely bay, on the south shore of which an old lumber shanty is visible, standing in a patch of raspberry bushes. We steer straight south round a narrow pen- insula that extends out from the west. On rounding its low rocky point we catch sight of a high hardwood mountain, a mile to the south, towering above the surrounding hills. This is the mountain we saw to the north of Island Lake, which is only between three and four miles south of our present position.

The head of White Trout Lake is at last before us at a distance of three-fourths of a mile. An open marsh [Grassy Bay] extends all across it, hemmed in on either side by high pine-clad hills. The view up the marsh is cut off by a thickly wooded island that lies right in the centre of the soft spongy ground. Round its base large quantities of cranberries may be gathered in the fall of the year. Steering along the north shore, we enter the river [Petawawa], a stream about six rods wide winding slowly along. At the distance of about two miles another, two-thirds its size, enters from the southwest. This one is the outlet of McIntosh's Lake, which lies a little over three miles to the west. Bending to the right, the main stream follows an arm or offshoot of the marsh for about a mile and a half farther, when the end of the marsh is reached. From this point it consists of a series of smooth stretches and short chutes up to the point we left a week ago below Misty Lake. It can be followed for several miles farther above that lake, when it spreads out into a network of lakes and small creeks that form its source.

The drier parts of the marsh are a favourite haunt of the moose in the fall, or during the fly season, and have at one time been well-timbered with cedar and tamarack, now nearly all dead and strewn on the ground or standing as bare white poles, their places being rapidly taken by large clusters of alders.

Before sunset we are back to camp discussing a hearty meal prepared of the same viands and in the same manner as yesterday's supper. Today we have been tracing the source of the Petewawa, one of the Ottawa's largest tributaries. We shall devote tomorrow to following its windings a few miles farther towards the north of White Trout Lake. We have frequently during the day seen large trout leaping up out of the water, and now find that the cook has his night line set. We will probably have the pleasure of testing their merits, as compared with their namesakes of the Muskoka, for breakfast.

The sun is scarcely an hour high when we are again merrily dancing over tiny wavelets, heading for the north end of the lake. We shall not return tonight, so a tent, blankets, and a two-day supply of provisions are taken along. We have not been disappointed in our anticipations of trout for breakfast, and found the quality quite up to our most sanguine expectations. In an hour or so we enter a little cove just beyond the burnt island seen from the camp. There, a short distance right ahead, is a newly built timber dam and slide—another evidence that the axe of the lumberman will be heard in these woods during the approaching winter. In five minutes more we are at the landing. It is but a few steps across to the foot of the portage, when we reach the head of a small pond. The fall is only a few feet. The dam has evidently been constructed for the sole purpose of keeping back the waters of the spring freshet, in order to retain them for use in floating the timber over some of the more shallow rapids farther downstream as the summer advances and the waters subside.

A five-minute paddle suffices to bring us to the foot of the pond, where there is another short chute with a few feet of fall, and the narrow raceway is overhung, and the water almost completely sheltered, by tall pines and hemlocks. At its foot lies a deep dark pool—a rare spot for trout. We are now in another lake. Away to the west at a distance of half a mile is a belt of rushes, behind which a hollow between the hills marks the channel of White Pine Creek [Tim River], which empties its waters through the rushes. That stream is famous for its trout and also as being a favourite haunt of the moose. A few strokes of the paddle, aided by the current from the falls, carry us out of the little cove and into a long narrow lake [Longer] stretching away almost due north, hemmed in at the lower end by a high mountain clothed like the others with hardwood and pine. On the east side, the hills rise only to a moderate elevation, and have already been depleted of most of their pine timber. On the west, the land attains a much higher elevation and becomes mountainous. The chain of waters here forms the boundary of a timber berth, the forest being still untouched on the west shore.

Arriving at the foot of this body of water, we see a narrow alder- and balsam-covered valley winding its course by the base of a mountain towards the northwest, through which another fine trout brook [Alder Creek] meanders to the mainstream. Here the waters become reduced to the dimensions of a river, and taking a sharp turn to the east, flow for a few chains through a grassy marsh, when they once more spread out for a quarter of a mile or so into a shallow pond. Another sharp bend almost at right angles, this time to the north, and we find ourselves in a deep, gently flowing stream eight or ten rods wide. In a few minutes another short portage is reached; then a few short stretches of smooth, still water where the stream spreads out a little; and a couple of short rapids down which we run the canoes, whence we enter Red Pine Lake [Redpine Bay].

At first sight it seems only another trifling expansion of the river, with a pine-clad bluff on our right front, but just before reaching this, a narrow neck of water leads into a beautiful rock-bound nook to the east, and the bluff turns out to be an island. Skirting along between the island and the west shore, we sight another lovely little gem of an island on which are a number of clusters of alders and a few graceful red pine. Stepping up the bank above the narrow strip of dark shingle, we find it literally covered with huckleberry bushes. Many large clusters of the blue fruit are already ripe, and like a band of school children we revel in their sweets. Here, as the sun is by now nearing the meridian, we conclude to have dinner, and the pail of tea is soon steaming on the mossy turf.

The body of the lake is now seen extending away to the east. The north shore is overhung by groves of the timber from which it derives its name. Moss-covered rocks and pine-crested mountains overshadow the numerous picturesque bays on the south side. After the usual noonday rest we again embark, and pursue our course northwards. Past several beautiful moss-covered isles and points, on emerging from a neck of deep water only a few chains wide we enter a large sheet of water stretching away far to the north and west. We head along the east shore, steering from point to point for some distance across the mouths of numerous small bays to where it bends in a graceful and regular curve towards the northeast. On nearing the north end, the side of a hill that has been burnt over is descried, and from this the lake has probably derived its name of Brûlé [Burntroot]. The shore still keeps trending to the east, the north side gradually closing in till the two almost unite, when the pent-up waters rush over a rocky bed on either side of a small island. We land at the head of the rapid, and following a well-beaten portage for five minutes, reach the foot. Here the Petewawa River flows in a majestic stream to the east.

We have traced it almost from its source, seen it gathering together its scattered waters, gradually increasing in volume till it now assumes the form of a deep swift river, and from this point continues on its way, collecting more waters from the large valley it drains, till finally it empties into the Ottawa ten miles northwest of the town of Pembroke. We shall now leave it and retrace our steps to Canoe Lake, and endeavour to find the source of another tributary of the Ottawa River—the Madawaska.

Here there are numerous traces of old campgrounds, as the river drivers have been detained here for some time each succeeding spring guiding the timber and sawlogs down the rough rapid at the outlet of the lake. As the sun is by this time low down in the west, we shall camp for the night, and explore the windings of the west shore on our way to the south again on the morrow.

CHAPTER 13 NOTES   *In this chapter, retracing the route from Burntroot Lake back to Canoe, Dickson describes a potential side trip (not actually part of the canoe voyage in the book) from Burnt Island Lake via Hailstorm Lake and Hailstorm Creek to Lake Opeongo in the watershed of the Madawaska River. This is not developed as a canoe route today, partly because of the long portages between Burnt Island and Hailstorm lakes. Dickson travelled the route in 1885 when he surveyed Bower Township and Lake Opeongo. Extensive bog along lower Hailstorm Creek is important wildlife habitat, "... one of the best spots in this whole section of country for duck shooting," Dickson notes—luckily for him no rangers then!*

*Lake Opeongo, largest in Algonquin Park, impressed Dickson by its beauty and by the quantity of pine timber there. It had been the scene of lumbering for at least 20 years when Dickson visited, and even an attempt at pioneer homesteading by Captain John Dennison and family. After the 82-year-old Dennison was killed by a bear in 1881, the surviving family members soon departed; the Fraser and McCoshen lumber company subsequently took over the old farm, near The Narrows, to use as a depot. Dickson no doubt welcomed the presence of this operating farm where he could obtain fresh provisions for his survey crew. In his survey report he describes it as "containing one hundred and twenty-one acres of clearing, well-fenced with large substantial dwelling house, barn, stables and other outbuildings .... On it is raised a large quantity of hay, oats, peas, potatoes and garden vegetables ... besides pasture for a large herd of cattle and a number of horses. This has also been an ancient Indian Fort, the old burying ground being still easily traced." Indians probably had an encampment there, but not likely a "fort."*

*The shooting of a deer swimming in Canoe Lake prompts Dickson to denounce what he considers the lack of sportsmanship demonstrated by many hunters, and the resulting scarcity of deer in some regions. The discussion is his strongest statement in the book on wildlife conservation, an issue that helped bring Algonquin Park into existence.*

## 13

## *More Explorations, and a Good Shot*

ON STEERING WESTERLY IN THE MORNING, WE NOTICE THAT WHILE
on our way north a large part of the lake was hidden from our
view by a number of small islands scattered over its surface, many
of which we mistook for the shore of the lake. The day is half
spent in steering in and out of the numerous bays that indent the
western shore, and admiring and speculating on the value of the
dense forest of large white pine that encircles it and extends away
to the west. The lake is crossed by the northern boundary of the
township of Bishop, the portion of its waters north of that lying in
the township of Osler.

By the time we retrace our way to the island on which we
dined yesterday, it is long past noon, but a remembrance of the
mass of luscious berries induces us to dine there again today. But
just before reaching it, we see a canoe rapidly approaching from
the east. A white puff of smoke rises from its bow, followed by the
crack of a rifle. This is taken as a signal that they wish to speak to
us, and firing a shot in reply, we lie still till they come up. They
turn out to be two of our own men we left in camp the preceding morning. They tell us they left camp in the early morning to
explore the deep bay extending easterly from the lumber shanty
on the north shore of White Trout Lake. On arriving near the foot
of the bay they found the end of a winter lumber road leading

northeasterly. Shouldering the canoe, they followed the road for a mile and a half, till it ended on the shore of another lake, when, launching the canoe, steering northwards and passing a narrow point, they found a large sheet of water extending apparently for miles to the east, its south shore rising into high hardwood ridges, and the north covered with red and white pine. It is named Lake La Muir. Beautiful hardwood mountains enclose its west shore.

Our men sailed through a cluster of islands past the mouth of a mountain stream finding its way through a gorge between the hills, and landed by the side of a swamp at the head of another bay in the northwest corner of the lake. Here they found a second lumber road, along which they travelled three-fourths of a mile, mostly through a large spruce swamp, when they struck the most easterly point of Red Pine Lake and began speculating whether it would be better to retrace their way to camp by the route they had come, or endeavour to find the river, by which they could return. Then our canoe was espied. As they had brought no lunch, they were tormented by the demon Hunger, which seems ever hovering round when one is inhaling the healthful bracing air of those woods and waters. They gladly join us at dinner.

The sun has gone down and darkness set in before our canoes are again launched on the waters of White Trout Lake. But as soon as we get past the little island, and are fairly out on the bosom of the lake, the campfire is distinctly visible even at a distance of nearly three miles; we quickly speed across the calm still waters to the landing. Soon we are agreeably engaged in discussing a plate of rich pea soup and trout with a top dressing of rice pudding, which the cook prepared in expectation of our return.

We indulge in an extra hour's sleep next morning, as the work of the last two days has been unusually hard and the boys were thoroughly tired out. But by eight o'clock everything is packed up, and we retrace our way to the mouth of Otter Slide Lake

Creek. We find it tedious, as well as very laborious, paddling and pushing up the shallow stream, for the water has perceptibly fallen since we descended. It is drawing towards the close of the second day ere we cross the height of land and again emerge on the shore of Island Lake. We had intended to cross to the foot of it this evening, but a stiff westerly gale impels us to retire a few rods into the woods and pitch camp for the night.

If time permitted, we might steer southerly across a couple of small bays on the east shore, and landing on the east side of a small islet, follow a surveyor's line running away eastwards. In a mile and three-fourths we would make the shore of a pond [Crossbill Lake]. Crossing this, and passing over a hill about half a mile farther on, we would arrive at another body of water named Hailstorm Lake. Launching out on its waters, and steering eastwards for half an hour, we would arrive at its outlet, a stream meandering through a spruce swamp [Hailstorm Creek]. Slowly working our way down this for a mile and a half, we would cross the east boundary of the township of McLaughlin and enter the newly surveyed township of Bower. A little over a mile farther we would find the stream joined by another from the north. It is now a good-sized but sluggish brook flowing through an open marsh, in many places the water completely covered by the broad leaves of the water lily, and one of the best spots in this whole section of country for duck shooting.

After an hour's paddle, rounding the last of its numerous sharp bends, the largest body of water we have yet seen would lie spread out before us, stretching in deep bays away to the north and east, and hemmed in by majestic heavily timbered mountains. Bending our course easterly along its high south shore, in a little over an hour we would pass into another large bay that extends to the southwest; then gliding through a cluster of islands, and steering southerly along the east shore, we would see another large body of water stretching far away to the southwest. Still tracing the east shore, at the end of another mile we would turn suddenly to the north through a neck of deep swift-flowing water, scarcely three rods wide, and in a couple of minutes more the largest bay of all would open to view, stretching away to the north and east. Right ahead on the left would be seen a large farm with substantial log buildings and groups of cattle and horses. Landing, we would be informed that we were on the Great Opeongo Lake, and that this is the depot of the lumbering firm Messrs. F&M.

Ascending a slight elevation, we would find ourselves on a narrow neck of land where we could see the magnificent sheet of water stretching far both to the east and west, studded here and there with pine-clad islets literally blue with huckleberries. We would be standing by the side of an old Indian burying ground, but the hand of the Paleface has defaced, removed, or destroyed all relics that would make it historically interesting. Beside the defaced grave of the aborigines, a pine slab marks the last resting place of a Mr. D, the pioneer of this section, who was killed a few years ago by a bear on the shore of the creek we just descended. But as time will not permit, we must for the present forgo the pleasure of a visit to the Great Opeongo.

Towards the close of the next afternoon we again breast the waters of Canoe Lake, heading for the old campground where we shall spend tomorrow, the Sabbath. Scarcely have the tents been pitched when an object is seen sailing out from behind the north end of the island, heading for the shore to the west of the inlet. At first sight it is taken for a loon, but as it is moving swiftly and steadily forward, the field glass is brought to bear, and the sharp nose and long ears of a fine doe are revealed. A canoe is instantly manned, and two of us are off in pursuit. She is well-nigh a mile away—we will have to strain every muscle to overtake her before she reaches land. As we are moving in a line almost at right angles to her course, we are within sixty rods before she discovers our approach. Then she dashes away at double her former speed. We must hasten, for she is now well in towards the shore, but we rapidly approach and dash across right in front of her. In couple of minutes more she would have been in shallow water, when a few bounds would have placed her out of danger and beyond pursuit. She wheels sharply round and heads for another point; but she is now completely at our mercy, and can be guided in whichever direction we choose.

After heading her off a few times, and watching the motions of her graceful tapering limbs in the water—the thought of accomplishing her destruction is too deeply seated in our minds for us to take any notice of the large, liquid, soft, pleading eyes—we steer up behind her till the canoe almost touches her quarters, and discharge a load of No. 3 shot into the back of her head. She floats lifelessly by our side. As we look at the finely shaped but drooping head, the protruding tongue, and the blood oozing from the nostrils and dyeing crimson the pure waters of the lake, a feeling of shame comes over us at the cowardly manner in which we have accomplished her destruction. We wonder how persons calling themselves sportsmen can go out day after day and idly lie on the edge of some bay or point, listening for the baying of the hound that heralds the approach of the harmless animal fleeing to this her only harbour of refuge; watch the graceful form leap into the water, imagining herself now safe from the bloodthirsty pursuers; watch till she is sufficiently far from shore to preclude the possibility of her return ere he gets within striking distance. He has only to exert his strength for five or ten minutes with the paddle, when the poor dumb brute is helplessly at his mercy, as completely in his power as the fettered sheep is in that of the butcher, and then to call this *sport!* Rare sport, indeed! If this is not pot hunting, then the word is a misnomer.

If the hunter desires real sport, sport where the game will have some chance for life, and where man's intelligence and endurance is pitted against the instinct and endurance of the denizens of the woods, he should dispense with the use of the hounds. Let him shoulder his rifle and go off alone into the woods. Let him train the feet to step lightly over rustling leaves and avoid fallen limbs, the ear to detect the various sounds peculiar to the woods so as to distinguish the movements of an animal from the creaking of one tree upon another or the rustling of the winds. Let him train the eye to detect the whisking of a tail, the flop of an ear, or the movement of a limb, and to discern the dun form from the surrounding timber and the antlered head from an upturned root; and, lastly, let him train the hand to make a quick and steady shot.

When the hunter has bagged the game by this proper method of hunting, he will feel that he has earned it, and that to track and bring down the wily buck in his native wilds is a feat any huntsman may be proud of. He will find that venison killed in this manner is a very different article from that produced by the carcass of a deer chased at full speed for several hours till its blood is at fever heat, then suddenly plunged into the ice-cold water of the lake and slaughtered before the body has had time to cool down to its normal condition.

There is also another method of deer-hunting with dogs, quite as objectionable as that of killing them in a lake, known as "shooting on the runways." Deer have almost invariably some particular spot for crossing a swamp, going over or round a hill, or course for swimming a lake or river. These crossings, where deer are plentiful, frequently assume the form of well-beaten paths that may be followed for miles. In many instances a number of them converge to form one large runway. In early morning a companion is sent into the woods with the dogs to start the game, while the other, gun in hand, takes his station at some well-known spot on the runway behind a tree or log. The approach of the deer is heralded by the baying of the hounds, and finally it is seen dashing along at full speed, intent only on escaping from its pursuers without paying any attention to danger ahead. The hunter can station himself as to be able almost to touch the animal as it rushes past, or, if it is a short distance off, a sudden whistle or shout will bring it to a standstill to look for the new danger, when in either case the hunter has a pot shot. In this case he has not even the labour of a short paddle to get within shooting distance, but has simply to stand still till the affrighted animal rushes into the ambush.

If deer were only slaughtered by the still hunter, there would be little necessity for game laws to protect them, and they would not, as they are now, be driven to the outskirts of the settlements, for there are enough of uncleared wild lands in all the northern counties in Ontario—lands unsuited for agricultural purposes—to form excellent game preserves. Were it not for this chasing with dogs, deer would be still as numerous in the settlements as they were before, as they are safer there from their natural enemies, the wolves.

As the slain deer furnishes an abundance of fresh meat for the table, there is no setting of the night line this evening. During the forenoon of the next day an excursion to the old campground on the island reveals a large quantity of ripe huckleberries, and the cook prepares a large roly-poly with some for supper.

CHAPTER 14 NOTES   *Marooned on an island in a storm-tossed Algonquin lake—not so bad when the island is covered with ripe blueberries!
Many a canoe tripper can appreciate Dickson's predicament in this chapter: returning from an excursion southwards to Ragged Lake, he arrives
at the foot of the Ragged–Smoke Lake portage only to find large waves
pounding into the bay at the south end of Smoke. Dickson attempts the
lake anyway in an effort to reach camp at the north end (not far from the
present Smoke Lake wharf site), but is forced ashore on Molly Island.*

*With purple tongues they eventually escape, and make a long north-
easterly portage, via Mizzy Lake, over the height of land to Source Lake
in the headwaters of the Madawaska River. Dickson considered this
portage—no longer used—a principal connection between the Oxtongue
and Madawaska, but the shortest and usual route from Smoke is via
Little Island Lake (the Mizzy Lake nature trail now follows part of
Dickson's portage). From Source the party descends the fledgling Madawaska River, known as the Little Madawaska above Tanamakoon Lake.*

*In his 1880 Peck Township report Dickson says he named Source
Lake (the uppermost large lake on the Madawaska; the true source lake
is actually Owl, 3 kilometres to the north). He may also have named
several others on the Algonquin highlands during his township surveys,
including Maggie (possibly after his wife, Margaret), Linda, Misty, Tea,
Head, Hailstorm, Cache, and Smoke (smoke from a fire on Molly
Island may have inspired the latter). His maps or reports contain the first
record of these and other names, but in some cases Dickson was likely
setting down names used by local trappers, with whom he often talked.
Dickson himself is honoured on the Algonquin map by Dickson Township and, indirectly, by Dickson Lake within it.*

*Dickson notes the canoe route leading from Ragged Lake southwest
to Hollow (Kawagama) Lake. As the distance is 20 kilometres—a third
of that portaging—it would be a feat to do it in the half day suggested.*

*Lack of fresh fruit and vegetables in their diet must have made blue-
berries an especially mouthwatering treat for the Algonquin surveyors.*

## 14

# A Gale, and the Source of the Madawaska

ANOTHER BRIGHT MORNING, AND ERE THE SUN IS TWO HOURS ABOVE the horizon we speed swiftly across the calm surface of Canoe Lake into the southeast bay, then trudge with stooping heads over half a mile of comparatively smooth portage to Smoke Lake. The camp is pitched on its shore: we shall spend the day tracing its headlands and bays, and also having a look at Ragged Lake, which lies only a short distance beyond its southern end.

Smoke Lake lies nearly due north and south, its extreme length being a little over three miles. Immediately west of the landing, a bay extends for half a mile to the outlet, which, as previously observed, empties into Tea Lake. The land round the north end is not very undulating, but about halfway up, a hardwood mountain on the west, and another almost directly opposite on the east side, tower high over the surrounding country. There are a few small islands, covered with pines and huckleberry bushes, scattered over its surface. Two deep bays directly opposite each other near the south end give the lake the appearance of a large rudely-shaped cross. It gradually narrows in the south into a small lily-covered bay where a brawling brook tumbles in over a mass of large boulders. This affords another favourite haunt for trout.

Ascending a short rugged portage, we encounter a small pond, on crossing which another five-minute climb brings us to the shore of Ragged Lake, and we are quickly skimming over its waters. A high pine-capped mountain lies directly a short distance ahead. On emerging from the little bay at the outlet, the water is seen extending away to the east; the mountain, when approached, turns out to be an island with a narrow channel between it and the west shore. Passing through this, we wind along the high western shore nearly due south. The lake extends in a number of small bays away to the east. On our right, a narrow strip of young poplars, with tall blackened trunks towering high above them, attests the presence a few years ago of a bush fire. On approaching a point on the west side, we pass out of the township of Peck into the township of Livingstone. In a few minutes more the shore turns abruptly to the west, where a broad belt of water extends south to a large tamarack swamp, behind which is a background of lofty pine-clad mountains. Approaching the west end, we turn north through a short narrows, re-entering Peck, and come upon another large sheet of water stretching away to the northwest, but so numerous are the little capes and islands that only a small part of it is visible at the same time. The sun is getting low before we have completed the circuit of its shores, and had a look at all its varied beauties. By the time we get back to the head of the portage at the outlet, darkness has set in.

Should the excursionist wish to visit Hollow Lake and return home by that route, let him steer into the end of the lake east of the high island. There he will find another trail, and following it south through a number of smaller lakes, he can reach that large and picturesque sheet of water in about half a day.

A stiff north wind now blows, and even if it were possible to cross the portage in the dark, it is questionable if we could face the heavy seas that must now be rolling into the head of Smoke Lake. We conclude to remain here for the night, and getting a big fire in full blaze, we make a light supper from the fragments left at lunch time. Judging from the appearance of the weather, we fear there may be rain during the night, so by the aid of the fire and cedar bark torches, a brush tent is soon constructed by the side of a big fallen pine. It will not by any means be quite waterproof should there be a heavy fall of rain, but it will partly protect us from the wet, and the abundance of dry limbs scattered within easy reach will enable us to keep a good large fire easily going. After the usual evening pipe, the fire is replenished and each disposes himself in the best manner he can for the night.

It is a gloomy morning. Heavy banks of dark leaden-coloured clouds move slowly towards the south. As soon as it is sufficiently light to enable us to find the trail, we are off, and the sun is barely up when we reach the foot of the portage. Though the wind has moderated considerably, a heavy swell still rolls into the mouth of the creek. Under ordinary circumstances we would not care to face it, but impelled by the urgent demand of empty stomachs, and the certainty they will have to remain in the same unsatisfactory state till camp is reached, we make the attempt. We are confident that the adjacent rapids and deep pools contain unlimited numbers of trout, of which we could improvise a rough but substantial breakfast. Before cooking, however, it is necessary they should first be caught, and by some oversight no one of the party has brought either a hook or line.

So we launch out at once and gently propel the little vessels across the big rolling waves. The canoes are light, and we ride like corks over the foam-crested swells, shipping only a very small quantity of water, but each succeeding ship drenches the face and arms of the man in the bow. As the bow rises on the approaching wave, the gunwale at the stern is almost on the level of the surface of the water. Our progress is exceedingly slow, for the canoe must have time to rise as she is caught by each succeeding wave; if she has not, she will plunge right into it and must inevitably swamp.

The wind, as is frequently the case at this season, increases in velocity as the sun attains a higher altitude, and ere we are half a mile on the way, a fierce gale blows. We dare not turn back for fear of getting swamped in the trough of the sea. Consequently, our only safe course is to steer straight ahead and assist the canoe with the paddles at the proper moment. We soon find that she is completely under control, and that by careful management we can weather the gale. Crouched in the bottom, so as to lower the centre of gravity, carefully and steadily we ply the paddles. Away straight ahead is an island towards which we lay our course. As we approach it, a creek is seen emptying in at the foot of a small bay on the east shore, while a belt of beaver grass on the west side marks the inlet of another—the outlet of a small lake [Swan] a mile away amongst the hills, from the deep clear waters of which many a splendid trout has been hauled.

The force of the wind and size of the waves gradually subside as we draw in under the lee of the island, and reaching a little cove we step on shore. Between the water we have shipped and the spray that has washed over us, we are pretty thoroughly drenched. The matches, however, have been kept dry, and in a few minutes we have a roaring fire of dry red pine limbs. One article of clothing is taken off and dried, then another removed and replaced by the dry one, this exchanging process continuing till everything is thoroughly dried; and were it not for the cravings of hunger, we should feel quite comfortable.

Stepping up from the shingly shore to the top of the island, our camp is plain in sight on the north shore. Away in the northeast, at the head of a deep bay, a large red object and two smaller ones are seen moving about. An application of the field glass reveals a doe feeding on the tender shoots of the young maple. With her on the yellow sand, two tiny, beautifully spotted fawns dance round and over each other like a couple of lambs.

The whole surface of the ground is blue with huckleberries. All hands are quickly at work in the enjoyment of a very fair substitute for breakfast. How much sweeter the fruit seems to the taste when newly plucked and eaten out of the hand than it does at any other time, no matter what else may be added to it!

Overhead, the tall slender trunks of the red pines, with their bushy tops, play round like whipstocks in the fierce gale tearing through their midst. All round our islet the angry waters toss and tumble in high white-crested waves. Breaking with a continuous roar on the shingly beach, they send great columns of spray high up amongst the trees in a manner that makes us thankful we were able to reach this goal before the gale rose to such fury, for none of our canoes could live a single minute in that rough sea. The sky is now perfectly clear—not a single speck of cloud. The whole day is spent in alternately eating berries, smoking, and sleeping.

Towards evening, the wind gradually begins to subside, but it is long after nightfall before the water has sufficiently quieted down to enable us again to put out. The smoke of the fire on the island having betrayed our presence to our friends at the camp, a huge fire is kept burning as soon as it is dark. By the light of this friendly beacon we guide our course to the camp, where in the enjoyment of a rich supper of venison steak, fresh trout, and delicious new-made bread, washed down by deep draughts of tea, the trouble and dangers of the preceding day and night are entirely forgotten, or make the subject of a jest. In less than an hour after landing all are fast in the arms of Morpheus.

The sun beams down from a cloudless sky as we emerge from the tent next morning. The gale of yesterday has completely subsided; perfect silence reigns. Today we shall move eastwards and endeavour to find the fountainhead of another of the great tributaries of the Ottawa. As is usually the case, but a brief space of time suffices to pack everything and load the canoes. The water is as smooth as a sheet of glass as we skirt round a low rocky point and cross a deep bay northeast of the camp.

A dozen yards north of a small belt of rushes, which marks the outlet of a small creek, a few blazed trees denote the end of another portage. This will be the longest carry we have yet had: to guard against a possible thundershower, one of the tents is erected to protect our goods while we are gone with a load. It is well-nigh two miles by the winding path before we shall again be enabled to make use of our canoes. Away with laden shoulders and stooping heads we march up the valley of the little creek. We proceed at a good swinging pace, for by this time we have become inured to our work, and are able not only to take a much heavier pack, but also to carry it much farther without resting than we could when we first started. After about a mile, now on one side of the creek and then on the other, we emerge on a long beaver meadow extending for nearly half a mile to the east. By our side is an old and dilapidated beaver dam. Were the beavers still here, the long bed of grass before us would be a lake, and would save three-fourths of a mile of portage; but all the industrious little animals have long since been destroyed by the ruthless hand of the trapper. The decayed dam, the gnawed stumps of the trees on which he fed, and the old beaver house, are all that now remain to indicate his former presence.

The trail leads through the tall grass to a timbered point jutting out from the north side, on reaching which the meadow is seen spreading out northwards to a spruce swamp. Away on the south side, a pine-crested mountain at least three hundred feet high rears its lofty head against the blue cloudless sky. Another quarter of a mile to the east a small lake [Mizzy] basks in the bright sunshine, its deep clear waters faithfully mirroring the tall grass on its shores and the mountain in the background. It lies directly in our path. As it will take all day to get the baggage up to this point, and as there is no high ground nearer the water, the tent brought along with us is set up here, and the packs are undone and stowed inside. After winding the tumplines round the shoulders, we retrace our steps to Smoke Lake, where our cook has a substantial dinner awaiting us. By sunset everything is across the portage, stowed away, and supper is over.

As usual, the sun is scarcely well above the horizon before we are astir next morning, and in another hour we are wending our way by the side of the small outlet to the boggy shore of the lake. Suddenly a beautiful otter springs out of an old beaver house, and with two or three graceful leaps plunges into the water. At a distance of a few rods from shore his round bullet head shoots above the surface. He surveys us for perhaps half a minute, then as suddenly as he rose he ducks down again, and we see him no more.

A few minutes paddle takes us across the twenty-five chains of lake, where a short time is spent picking green cranberries that grow thickly on the few rods of marsh intervening between the water and the woods. Here again a well-cut portage is found extending easterly; in less than ten minutes we stand by the side of a large body of water spreading out towards the east. A few minutes afterwards we are skimming over its deep, blue waters. The west shore is formed by a number of little bays, while a short distance out are a few small but lovely islands. The course is shaped nearly due east. The south shore is rather low, with only a few knolls rising more than a few feet above the surface of the water. The timber is a mixture of nearly all the varieties peculiar to the country. On the north, at a short distance from the water, is a high maple-covered hill. About a mile from the west shore, on the north side behind a few small rocky islets, a large creek slowly winds in through a tamarack swamp. Away to the east the land rises into heavily wooded mountains.

Half a mile from the east end, a small grassy point juts out from the south side nearly opposite a large and heavily timbered island. A few chains farther we cross the east boundary of Peck into the township of Canisbay. Rounding a point, still another bay is seen stretching for a quarter of a mile to the south. Its sides are completely covered with fallen timber, leaving only a narrow space of clear water in the middle. At its foot, by an old beaver dam, a large creek tumbles over a rocky bed in a southeast direction. We have found another river, for this is the headwater—the very fountainhead—of the Madawaska. This is Source Lake, the most westerly of its waters. The last portage is the dividing ridge between it and the Muskoka.

A fifteen-minute tramp brings us to the foot of the portage. It is all level or downhill this time, and for most of the distance we hear the creek tumbling down the rocky ledge a few rods to the left. We emerge on its shore at the foot of the rapid, at the head of a beaver meadow almost completely overgrown with alders. The stream is scarcely big enough for one canoe to pass at a time. It is only a short distance to the next portage, and the remainder of the day is spent alternately pulling and paddling down the narrow creek and carrying our baggage across the rough portages. At the head of each portage is an old dilapidated beaver dam. The land rises at a short distance on either side into high ridges, all densely covered with pine, hemlock, and hardwood timber. The black muddy shore of each little pond is literally covered with deer and moose tracks; one moose is seen at a distance dashing off through the alders, heading for the high dry land.

We finally halt for the night at the foot of the last portage on this part of the stream ere we emerge into the next lake, where there is an old campground. We always prefer pitching camp if possible on an old camping place, as it saves the trouble of clearing off the ground and there are generally old tent poles lying round that can be utilized.

CHAPTER 15 NOTES   *The Dickson Algonquin adventure is now well into its fourth week—mid-August, probably—with the party travelling the upper reaches of the Madawaska River, the largest tributary of the Ottawa River on the Ontario side. This is country Dickson explored in 1882 while surveying Canisbay Township. He didn't revisit these waterways before writing his book.*

*Below Cache Lake on the Madawaska, the party once again leaves the island of virgin forest straddling the height of land, and enters the domain of the lumbermen. The cutters, however, have not been active here for some years—a lull before the final assault on the pineries of western Algonquin. Dickson reported considerable pine in the upper Madawaska watershed, even in areas where logging had occurred.*

*Dickson likely named Cache Lake, in consequence of locating his store camp there during the township survey. In the book, but not in his survey notes, he spells it Caché: this has led to speculation that the name was originally Lac Caché—Hidden Lake—which does fit with its geography. But the accent may be an affectation, for it appears also in the book, improperly, on "cachéd." (The accents are omitted in this edition.) Still wilderness when Dickson saw it, except for a hunter's (more likely trapper's) cabin, Cache Lake soon underwent great transformation: raised water levels behind a lumbering dam; railway tracks, bridges, and trestles on the Booth line (1896); the new Algonquin Park headquarters (1897); and in 1908 the Highland Inn hotel and the Northway children's camp. Numerous cottages have been built on its shores as well.*

*Dickson considered Head Lake "the head" of that branch of the Madawaska (Head Creek); actually, Head Creek rises in Bonnechere Lake several kilometres to the south—beyond the territory he surveyed.*

*Near the end of this final chapter Dickson offers a rather fanciful account of Indian life on the Algonquin highlands and, apparently, the Iroquois attack on Huronia in 1649. This is another example of material bearing little resemblance to Dickson's writing style, and almost certainly penned by someone else.*

## *We Finish Our Explorations, and Our Holiday*

FROM THIS POINT, THOUGH BOTH VERY CROOKED AND NARROW, THE creek is sufficiently deep to enable us to make constant use of the paddle. In fifteen minutes, on emerging from a bed of tall grass, we find ourselves in another lake [Tanamakoon] which lies away to the west, a short distance into the township of Peck. We keep along its east shore, across the mouth of a few small bays, and in a little over half a mile arrive at the outlet, guarded at the distance of a few rods by a small island. Steering slowly through big trunks of floodwood and large stones for a short ways, we reach a sluggish stream about four rods wide with barely water enough in some parts to float us. Its shores are lined with water lilies and fallen timber, with an occasional tall white trunk extending halfway across, round which we carefully pick our way.

Rounding a bend to the left, we see the stream in the distance widening out into a small lake or pond, while a few rods in front a narrow riband of ferns and beaver grass spans the creek. This is another old and deserted beaver dam, which when in good repair must have dammed the water back as far as the foot of the last portage—this no doubt made the small beaver meadow between the end of the portage and the lake. The top of the dam now stands between two and three feet above the surface of the water. A narrow cut, large enough to admit a canoe, has been made in it near the centre. Through this we pass, and in a few minutes we are in deep clear water. This is no small pond, but Cache Lake.

A lovely birch-clad island lies right before the mouth of the creek; on its west end we see a hunter's cabin. The water extends away past a high point on the south side to the southeast, and also to the north of the island both northerly and easterly. We steer down the south side. Gradually a large body of water unfolds to view, stretching away to the north past the east end of the island, and also in two long bays to the southwest, with a bold, rocky, but straight south shore, till it rounds up in a beautiful bay in the southeast. South of the lake the country is rugged and mountain-ous, and heavily timbered with pine and hemlock. On getting within three-fourths of a mile of the east shore, we turn to the northeast down a narrow neck of water between a peninsula on the west and, on the east, a high mountain that extends in dark granite cliffs to unknown depths beneath the surface. Arriving at the end of this channel, another bay opens out, extending to the east and south, leaving another small peninsula on our right. At the east end of the bay a pile of floodwood denotes the outlet, and as we draw near, a roaring of water indicates the presence of a fall or chute.

The portage is on the south side of the stream, when, transfer-ring the loads from the canoes to our shoulders, at the end of a quarter of a mile we re-embark in smooth water below the rapids. The volume of water is now very much larger than above Cache Lake. Gliding smoothly and swiftly down the stream, in a few minutes we are again on the track of the Ottawa lumberman. A cluster of old lumber shanties is passed, and the stumps of large pine that have been cut are thickly studded along the banks: this is the most westerly point to which their operations have extended on the Madawaska River.

A short distance below the shanties we enter a long narrow

marsh hemmed in on either side by high rugged mountains. The water is beautifully clear. We glide smoothly in the gently flowing current with only an occasional dip of the paddles. Presently the marsh is seen extending beyond the point of a high mountain to the south. Our stream also takes a southerly turn. In a few minutes another [Head Creek], more than half its size, empties into it from the southwest; up this we wend our way. In half an hour we arrive at a little rapid, where the cookery is unpacked and dinner eaten.

A portion of our loads, not needed for the night, is cached at this point, and carrying over the short and shallow rapid, we continue our route against the stream. At the head of the rapid we enter another long narrow marsh; at the end of a mile the high dry land again closes in on the water. The channel of the stream is divided into two parts. That on the west side is a rough broken chute, the water dashing down amongst the stones. Across this are the remains of an old dam, roughly constructed but strong, built by the lumberers to throw the water into the other channel, at present perfectly dry. This one is an inclined furrow in the granite rock, in shape like a huge trough, its sides and bottom smooth as if made by a plane.

In a few rods more the mountains again recede on either side of the stream, leaving between them another marsh, through which the channel winds its devious course. In half an hour the high lands once more close in on the water, and we step on shore at the foot of another stony chute. A short portage brings us to the head, where we encounter the remains of another dam. We are at the foot of what seems to be a small pond. After embarking, a few strokes of the paddle carry us up to and beyond a small point on the south side, when a beautiful sheet of water is seen stretching towards the south. This is Head Lake; here we conclude to camp for the night.

Landing the loads, while our men prepare the tents we take a paddle round the silent shores and look into the small picturesque bays. This lake is a perfect gem, and completely mountain-locked. Away in the southwest, halfway down its southern shore, a creek some two or three yards wide enters; a smaller one rolls in down a mountainside; while in the extreme east a small marsh, with a narrow valley between the hills, denotes the presence of a third. Each of these has its source in a small lake or beaver pond, and this is the head of the second stream that forms the nucleus of the waters of the Madawaska.

This lake, like all the others, literally teems with trout. Its northern shore has been well-nigh denuded of its pine timber, but on the south the dense primeval forest is still untouched. We have a lovely spot for our camp on the point southwest of the dam. The young crescent moon with its lights and shadows gleams brightly through the trees, and the mountain and pines of the north shore are faithfully and beautifully mirrored in the deep clear waters. The perfect silence is broken only by the shrill weird cry of a couple of loons.

By ten o'clock next day we are back to where we dined and left a portion of our loads on the way up. Beyond the forks the stream, now beginning to assume the dimensions of a river, pursues its zigzag course through the marsh. After another mile we arrive at the foot of the marsh, and the hard land approaches again to the side of the water. On the south, a few rods from the shore, a perpendicular cliff rears its head for at least one hundred feet skyward. Majestic red and white pine crown its top, these standing in a carpet of dun-coloured moss in which one sinks ankle-deep at every step, the whole surface almost blue with clusters of ripe huckleberries. From every crevice on the face of the cliff a small pine or cedar, bunch of ground hemlock, or small white birch maintains its position, looking healthy and vigorous in spite of the very limited quantity of soil that surrounds the roots.

Here there is another chute and remains of a timber dam, and a portage of four or five chains. For the next few miles the stream is an alternation of short rapids and smooth stretches of almost still water enclosed between high mountains, an occasional break in the hills affording egress to a small spring creek where we can enjoy a drink of ice-cold crystal water. We pass across many rare pools for trout, but our time is too limited to allow us to indulge in sport. We finally enter a bed of alders beyond which no timber is seen. After rounding a sharp bend and shooting past the last clump, we are suddenly rising and falling on the long steady swell produced by a northeast breeze on the Lake of Two Rivers.

Paddling a few rods out into the lake, we see another stream [North Madawaska River], fully as large as that we have just descended, winding in through a bed of rushes about ten chains to the north. It is from these two rivers the lake derives its name. Were we to follow this other river a few miles towards the northwest, we would pass numerous little ice-cold rivulets, and finally reach a point where the waters divide into two streams of equal size, the one winding its way from the northwest, the other from the northeast. Each one would again subdivide as we proceeded, the main branch growing steadily less, and each of the numerous rivulets draining some small gully or swamp, till the last is finally lost in an impassable bog or beneath a ledge of rock or root of some giant cedar or pine. The longest, and that which extends farthest towards the west, has its rise in the small lake [Crossbill] east of Island Lake.

The south shore of Lake of Two Rivers is a high maple-crested mountain. As is usually the case with the lakes in this section of country, it has a narrow fringe of cedar and balsam along the edge of the water. On the north is a forest chiefly of white pine. About halfway down the north shore there is a deserted clearing with a dwelling house and barn. This was a few years ago the central depot of a large lumbering establishment, the distributing point whence the outlying camps were supplied. The lake is about two and a half miles long by one wide. Skirting along the south shore, we reach the outlet, a deep swift river flowing southeasterly.

We launched our frail canoes on the broad bosom of the Muskoka River and ascended that stream, finding it gradually growing smaller as we passed one brook and lake after another, till finally we reached its source in Island Lake. Thence we crossed the height of land and tapped the waters of the Petewawa, followed its winding course and gazed on the varied beauties of the lovely lakes forming its source. When we found it assumed the dimensions of a large river, we bid it adieu and retraced our steps.

In like manner we crossed the watershed between the Muskoka and Madawaska, explored and viewed the headwater creeks and lakes of the latter, till we found them uniting into a deep, wide stream that performs the double function of draining the surrounding country of its superabundant water and forming also the highway down which the wealth of timber produced by the vast surrounding forest is conveyed to market. For three-quarters of a century the Madawaska has annually borne upon its bosom a rich freight of valuable timber, cut and drawn onto its icy covering during the preceding winter, then delivered down to the mighty Ottawa. Borne onwards by those waters, a portion of it has been manufactured into sawn lumber by the mills along the course, the residue loaded on ocean vessels at the city of Quebec and thence conveyed to all quarters of the globe.

As we stand by the shore of the swift-flowing river, the scenes of our early youth are recalled vividly to the mind's eye. Far away, near where its waters mingle with those of the Ottawa, our early youth was passed. We recall many happy hours spent by the side of its turbulent rapids, bathing and fishing in its swift waters, gathering the ripe berries that grew abundantly along its rugged shores in early autumn, or tracking the deer in the deep cedar swamps and along the rocky gulches during the first snows of winter.

But the track over which we have passed is famous for scenes other than those produced by inanimate nature. Far in the remote ages of the past, those valleys and woods were thickly peopled by the red man. And those waters were one of the highways by which the Iroquois of the Ottawa marched to make war on their hereditary enemies, the Hurons. One party ascended the Madawaska, another the Petewawa, and uniting their forces in Canoe or Tea Lake, together they descended the Muskoka and attacked the villages scattered along the shores of its lower lakes; thence, marching overland, they carried death and destruction to the shores of Couchiching and Simcoe while the defenders were off repelling the attack of other war parties assailing them by the way of French River.

Could the veil in which the unwritten past is enshrouded be withdrawn, scenes of valour, scenes of heroism, and scenes of cruelty and blood would be beheld, equal to any told in the histories of the Old World. But the aborigines of this continent were utterly without the simplest forms of literature, and the history of the tribes has been preserved only in legendary lore handed down from sire to son. They had no Homer to write the history of their sieges, no Ossian to sing of the valour of their chieftains, the fierceness of their combats, or the beauty of their daughters, and there is now no Byron to bewail their fallen greatness.

One almost expects when crossing the narrow portage to meet a line of plumed and painted warriors treading noiselessly with moccasined feet along the winding path, to see them speeding swiftly across the tossing waters of the lakes, or along the silent reaches of the rivers. No cumbersome provision or ammunition train accompanied the army of the red man. The scalping knife, the stout elm bow, and the glittering tomahawk were his only weapons, the quiver full of arrows slung behind the shoulder his only ammunition. The forest and water afforded abundance of his frugal food. The naked earth was to him a luxuriant couch, the foliage of the woods and canopy of heaven an ample covering.

In those shadowy dells the Indians were born, in those they lived, in those they died and were buried. They knew no other world than their native forests. They hankered after neither wealth nor fame. Their only ambition was to excel in the chase or on the field of battle.

Here the dusky maidens viewed their graceful forms and bathed their shapely limbs in the crystal waters, and entwined their raven tresses with garlands of maple leaf and silvery birch.

Round those pine-clad mountains the buckskin-clad hunter tracked the lordly moose and elk, or chased them in his light canoe across the still waters of the lakes, and sent the quivering arrow into their vitals.

Beneath those spreading cedars the youthful hunter brought the trophies of the chase, the painted warrior the spoils of the battle, and laid them at the door of the wigwam as proof of their prowess, with which to woo and win their youthful brides. And in those moonlit dells as daring deeds of chivalry were wrought and as tender tales of love told as ever were sung by a Scott or a Burns.

Kind reader, our task is ended. When we began this little book our only ambition was to attract the attention of lovers of romantic scenery to those wilds, which, though within such easy distance, are almost unknown. But to see this section of country in all its varying beauty, one would have to visit it during the depth of winter when the forest is clothed in its mantle of white and the waters of lake and river lie still and hushed beneath their icy covering; again in the early spring days when the buds of the grey woods unfold into the green leaf, the wimpling burn is a brawling brook, and the calm-flowing waters of the rivers are roaring torrents; and again in the fall of the year when the green leaves turn to red and golden yellow, and the ice-coated limbs of the trees glitter in the bright sunshine.

While we have endeavoured to describe some of its beauties, there are still other spots of equal loveliness in those dark woods, which the limited time at our disposal will allow us neither to visit nor illustrate. But at the close of our holiday we return to our labours amongst our fellow men invigorated and strengthened both in mind and in body.

# Bibliography

*Included here are the major sources consulted in writing the Introduction and chapter commentaries, as well as selected other books providing good coverage of the scenery and cultural and natural history of Algonquin.*

OTTELYN ADDISON, *Early Days in Algonquin Park* (Toronto: Mc-Graw-Hill Ryerson, 1974). The classic illustrated history by the daughter of early park ranger Mark Robinson.

RALPH BICE, *Along the Trail with Ralph Bice in Algonquin Park* (Toronto: Consolidated Amethyst, 1980). Colourful reminiscences by a former trapper and guide.

[WILLIS CHIPMAN], "James Dickson," Association of Ontario Land Surveyors *Annual Report of Proceedings* (v. 42, 1927, pp. 108-114). Biography, partly based on material written by Dickson.

JAMES DICKSON, Township survey reports, 1878-1885. Handwritten (photocopies in Algonquin Park archives). Edited versions were printed in Ontario *Sessional Papers*.

[JAMES DICKSON et al.], *Report of the Royal Commission on Forest Reservation and National Park* (Toronto, 1893).

G.D. GARLAND (compiler), *Glimpses of Algonquin: Thirty Personal Impressions From Earliest Times to the Present* (Whitney: Friends of Algonquin Park, 1989). A wonderful cross-section of accounts of Algonquin dating back to 1824, with commentary.

G.D. GARLAND, *Names of Algonquin: Stories Behind the Lake and Place Names of Algonquin Provincial Park* (Whitney: Friends of Algonquin Park, 1991).

GERALD KILLAN, *Protected Places: A History of Ontario's Provincial Parks System* (Toronto: Dundurn Press; Ministry of Natural Resources, 1993). Exhaustively researched; contains account of Algonquin history from political and management perspective.

GARY LONG, *This River the Muskoka* (Erin: Boston Mills, 1989). Includes history and geography of the Oxtongue River.

NIALL MACKAY, *Over the Hills to Georgian Bay* (Erin: Boston Mills, 1981). Illustrated account of the Booth railway.

RODERICK MACKAY, WILLIAM REYNOLDS, *Algonquin* (Toronto: Stoddart, 1993). Accurate, comprehensive history with beautiful, but unidentified, colour plates. See the chapter on surveying.

WILLIAM REYNOLDS, TED DYKE, *Algonquin* (Toronto: Oxford University Press, 1983). The first large-format Algonquin colour pictorial. Has useful captions.

MICHAEL RUNTZ, *Algonquin Seasons: A Natural History of Algonquin Park* (Toronto: Stoddart, 1992). A naturalist–photographer's perspective of Algonquin. Pictorial, with useful captions.

AUDREY SAUNDERS, *Algonquin Story* (Toronto: Ontario Department of Lands and Forests, 1947). The original history of Algonquin, much of it based on interviews with old-timers.

S. BERNARD SHAW, *Canoe Lake, Algonquin Park: Tom Thomson and Other Mysteries* (Burnstown: General Store, 1996).

DONALD STANDFIELD, LIZ LUNDELL, *Algonquin: The Park and its People* (Toronto: McClelland & Stewart, 1993). Colour plates and profiles of interesting Algonquin characters are its strong points.

RON TOZER, DAN STRICKLAND, *A Pictorial History of Algonquin Provincial Park* (Whitney: Friends of Algonquin Park, 1991). Another of many excellent and inexpensive Friends publications about the natural and cultural history of Algonquin.

# Index

```
———◼◼———
```

## ABOUT THE EDITOR

Gary Long trained and worked as a geographer, then turned to writing, but both careers gave him ample opportunity to indulge in his favourite activity: exploring and researching the waterways of the Muskoka–Algonquin region. In his book *This River the Muskoka* (1989) he examined the history and geography of many of the lakes and rivers James Dickson describes. Author of numerous articles focusing on the same countryside, he also wrote the chapter about the epic Gilmour log drive, which began in the headwaters of the Oxtongue River, for the book *Canoe Lake, Algonquin Park* in 1996. Gary has resided in Muskoka for most of his life.

A NOTE ON THE TYPE

This book is set in Bembo. Highly regarded for book work because of its readability and quiet elegance, Bembo is based on the classic typeface cut by Francesco Griffo in 1495 for Venetian publisher Aldus Manutius, and first used in Pietro Bembo's *De Ætna*. Griffo's design inspired the graceful "old style" faces that prevailed in Europe until the 18th century, and which, resurrected and refined, have again found great favour among book designers. Stanley Morison and staff at English Monotype Corporation created Bembo in 1929 as part of an ambitious programme to revive classic typefaces.

Book designed by Lorrie Szekat

*Printed and bound in Canada on acid-free paper by*
*Best Book Manufacturers Inc.*